You Are
SALT &
Light

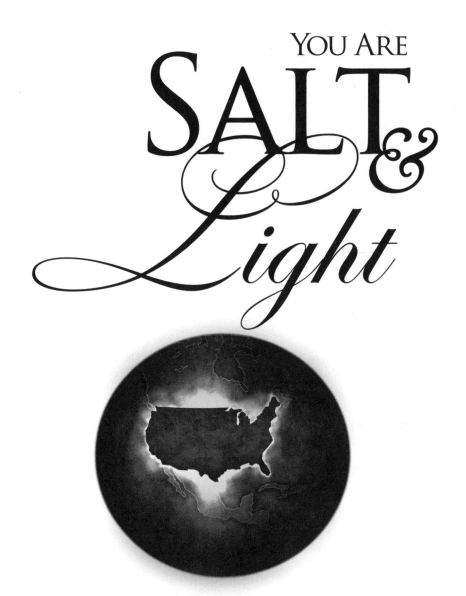

EQUIPPING CHRISTIANS
FOR THESE LAST DAYS

BOB

Copyright 2009
Revised with group and/or individual study questions from original Salt & Light
published in 2007.
Robert R. Fraley
All rights reserved
ISBN 978-0-9612999-9-6

Published by
Christian Life Outreach
P.O. Box 31129
Phoenix, Arizona 85046-1129
Phone: 866-998-4136, e-mail: xnlifeout@yahoo.com

www.bobfraleychristianlifeoutreach.com

Printed in the United States of America

Cover design by Paul Annan and Robin Black

ACKNOWLEDGEMENT

I wish to acknowledge and thank Dr. David Mains,
George Koch, Derald McDaniel and Mary Prether
for their work on this revised and edited version
of the original copy of *Salt & Light*.
This edition has been arranged for a 13 week
Bible study with questions for group discussion
and/or individual study.

CONTENTS

INTRODUCTION

What you read in this book will probably challenge much of what you've heard or read about Bible prophecy, particularly what Scripture says about America's future. Pray that God will give you discernment to evaluate what I am saying. Understanding these truths is key to comprehending the enemy's attack plan in these last days—and overcoming him.

These important spiritual concepts are foundational to a grasp of the prophetic Scriptures about America. In writing this book, I have presented the material in a specific order, so to avoid missing any key points, please read the book from beginning to end—don't "skip around." When you finish, you will understand the root cause of Satan's warfare in America and why, in this last generation, he has been so successful in tearing down our Christian values causing America to leave her first love.

～～～～

AMERICA, which had such a strong Christian foundation, has experienced an overwhelming increase in the spirit of selfishness, permissiveness, lawlessness and rebellion in this last generation. **WHY?**

Moral standards in America that were unthinkable 30-40 years ago have now become commonplace. **WHY?**

Drugs, crime and violence are huge problems. America has the largest prison population in the world. Our incarceration rate is more than seven times that of most other countries. **WHY?**

Since World War II the percentage of young Americans with biblical-based values has dropped from 65 to 4 percent. **WHY?**

Christian leaders and church members alike are falling into sexual sin. **WHY?**

Addiction to pornography has reached epidemic levels for both Christians and non-Christians. **WHY?**

The divorce rate has skyrocketed among both Christians and non-Christians in our country. **WHY?**

In the history of mankind, there has never been a society where moral values have deteriorated so drastically in such a short period of time as those of America during the past 50-60 years ... and that trend shows no sign of changing. Yet America has more Bible colleges and seminaries; churches and denominations; Christian books, tapes, and videos; evangelistic outreaches; Christian bookstores, TV and radio stations—than the rest of the world combined.

WE WILL NOT KNOW HOW TO OVERCOME THE ENEMY.

Respected Christian leaders have expressed concern that God's judgment is overdue for America. Nothing seems to have any effect on the problems we face, and the country continues in its sinful ways. What is going on? Why have all of our efforts failed? Why has Satan had so much success in his attacks against the church in America?

The answer is in God's Word! To quote Hosea 4:6, **"My people are destroyed** [defeated] **for lack of knowledge."** Christians **lack knowledge about how Satan is attacking the Body of Christ in these last days**. Until we comprehend the root cause of this warfare, we will not know how to overcome the enemy, and the spiritual defeat and moral decay will continue. That is why I have written this book!

Satan is well aware of America's great spiritual history. Our nation has been a key base for Christianity over the last 100-plus years. Therefore, seeing his time is short, the enemy has launched a vicious attack against American Christians. He plans to destroy every biblical standard we hold. Only when we understand his attack methods will we know why he is causing so much spiritual defeat in the Body of Christ. This is the only way we can prepare ourselves to stand against what will be the enemy's last offensive.

A few years ago there was a surge of interest in the end-times, but now it seems the subject has lost its appeal. Maybe this is because the earlier materials failed to prepare Christians by telling them how to be overcomers in these troubled times.

Most Christians are not spiritually prepared to stand against Satan's deceptive tactics. Many admit they do not understand the root cause of the rapid breakdown or how the enemy has conducted such a successful campaign of changing the moral values in our country.

Sadly, hundreds of thousands of Christians have been hurt in these encounters. Christian leaders are falling into sin, right along with lay-people. Materialism and greed have taken their toll. Most alarming is the fact that the spiritual decay process is spreading rapidly. We need to realize that we are living in one of the toughest times in history to be a committed Christian. Never before has our spiritual enemy had the ability to tempt so many people as our American society can through TV, radio, music, movies, the Internet, printed media and advertising.

No longer do you and I have to go out into the world in order to make contact with it. Its influence marches right into our homes and seeks us out! The Christian family has never felt the pull of a worldly society like what we contend with today. Americans are hit daily in every way imaginable to compromise biblical standards. We are living in the middle of a spiritual warzone, and too many Chris-

> WE ARE LIVING IN
> THE MIDDLE OF
> A SPIRITUAL WARZONE.

tians have become casualties. Dr. Billy Graham said a few years ago that, according to his research, at least 90 percent of all American Christians live defeated spiritual lives.

My entire career has been in the corporate business world, mostly as an executive. In 1997, I founded ALEXCO, a major manufacturer of high-tech aluminum extruded alloys for the aerospace industry. We hold a weekly meeting of managers and other personnel to review company performance. Corrective action is quickly implemented if an area of weakness is detected in a department. Just as Jesus taught, your fruit or performance is the sign of success or failure in whatever you do.

As we evaluate what has been produced in our nation during the last generation, we see the fruit of an evil work. <u>We cannot afford to hide our heads in the sand.</u> Fruit reveals truth! By looking at this we can see that America is headed in the wrong direction. We are in danger of spiritual bankruptcy!

It is time for Christians to take a stand! I know spiritual warfare is never a favorite subject to discuss. War is very stressful. It can be expensive and dangerous. It requires skill and discipline to emerge victorious, much less unscathed. That is why few of us seek out conflict. It puts us at risk. Therefore, our human tendency is to avoid it unless we are pushed beyond a reasonable limit. I believe you will agree with me—that time has come!

> UNDERSTAND BOTH THIS WARFARE AND THE DECEPTIVE TACTICS THAT SATAN IS USING.

As Christians in America today, we really don't have a choice. We are involved in this warfare whether we like it or not. There is a spiritual battle taking place to destroy the biblical standards that most Americans once honored and lived by. We cannot avoid the effects of this battle. The worldly standards that are being promoted are just too strong and far-reaching.

Most believers go into the world everyday unprepared for the snares of Satan's worldly system. We have not developed a plan for counterattacking. We need to understand our opponent's tactics before we can know how to counter them.

<u>We need a specific corrective-action plan.</u> If we don't quickly develop one, we will continue to fall away from God's special calling to us as

a people. This is what Satan wants—to defeat God's purpose. It is why he has launched such a heavy attack against our country.

Every day we hear about the war against terror. However, few Americans, including Christians, are knowledgeable about the spiritual warfare taking place, even though it has been more detrimental to our country. My purpose in writing this book is to share the knowledge we need to understand both this warfare and the deceptive tactics that Satan is using.

Every born-again Christian is called to act in a way that goes against conventional wisdom, social expediency and the popular will. We have a mission to fulfill and a responsibility to make our country, and the world, a better place by preserving all that is good as given us through God's Word. We are to be people who put the Kingdom of God first. That is what being **"salt and light"** is all about! But we can only do this if we are prepared. This book will give you the knowledge you need to prepare yourself to stand against the enemy's spiritual attacks in these last days, and it will help you develop the spiritual character needed to be **"salt and light"** in the face of today's tremendous pressures.

A Personal Word

My wife, Barbara, and I are devoted to family values. In 2007 we celebrated our 50th anniversary. We have three sons of our own, and back in 1969 the Lord called us to take six children into our home whose parents had been killed in a car accident. Being fairly young, we were dependent on the Lord in raising our expanded family.

As we trained these children, many things began to happen that made it obvious the Lord was directing us in a miraculous way. Not only can we testify to this, but so can others who were close to our situation. Jesus said, **"You did not choose me, but I chose you to go and bear fruit—fruit that will last. Then the Father will give you whatever you ask in my name"** (John 15:16).

One of the major things He did was to open our eyes to the warfare Satan had launched for the hearts and minds of the American people.

This insight was the foundation the Lord used to guide us in raising godly children in an increasing godless society. We now have 62 in our family including spouses, grandchildren and great-grandchildren, and every one, except for the few who are too young, has made a commitment to serve the Lord.

Though we were quite busy with nine children, I was convicted to share the things the Lord was teaching my wife and me. Since the early 1970s this directive motivated me to research America's secular and spiritual history. I also began to study the Scriptures about the characteristics of the Christian life and prophecies about the last days.

My study convinced me that Christians are not being taught how our spiritual enemy will attack them in the end-times. If we want to avoid suffering a major defeat, such an understanding is vital. These prophecies give us the insights we need to stand against the enemy and fulfill our **God-given mission to be salt and light**. What you will read will challenge your thinking. I trust it will also open your eyes to the battle we are facing, and it will show you the way forward to victory.

If Bible prophecy is true—and we know that it is—then it must be our priority to learn how the enemy is attacking the Christian community in these last days. I was recently called by the Lord to start Campaign Save America to inform people about this spiritual warfare. (Visit our Web site, www.bobfraleychristianlifeoutreach.com). The mission of this campaign is to preserve God's special calling for His people in America in these last days. America is in danger!

The Bible says that as it was in the days of Noah, so will it be in our day (see Luke 17:26-30). **"By faith Noah, when warned about things not yet seen, in holy fear built an ark to save his family"** (Hebrews 11:7). This book will provide you the materials you need to build a spiritual ark for you and your family as you prepare for what's ahead.

Bob Fraley

CHAPTER ONE

AMERICA'S SPECIAL CALLING

I believe that from its beginnings God had a special place in His heart for our nation. Even a brief glance at our history confirms this.

To understand the way God has worked in America, we should first recall the history of Israel. Most of us are familiar with the Old Testament account. Scripture certainly reveals a special place in God's heart for His chosen people. It is clear that God often intervened in their story so that His mission would be accomplished. Unfortunately, the Jewish people regularly got caught up in the ways of the world, and as a result fell away from serving the God of Abraham.

I believe our country's spiritual development confirms that we, too, have experienced a special calling from God—perhaps not to the same degree as Israel's, but our spiritual heritage is unique compared to that of most other countries. Except for Israel, I believe there has never been another nation where God has so directly intervened as He has in the spiritual development of America. Let me share some examples.

ILLUSTRATION NUMBER ONE

It is common knowledge that Columbus discovered America in 1492. What is not so well-known is his call from God to venture out and discover the New World. An article in the October 1971 issue of *Presbyterian Layman* included this translated excerpt from the explorer's own writings, *The Book of Prophecies*:

"It was the Lord who put into my mind (I could feel his hand upon me) the fact that it would be possible to sail from here to the Indies. All who heard of my project rejected it with laughter, ridiculing me. There is no question that the inspiration was from the Holy Spirit, because He comforted me with the rays of marvelous inspiration from the Holy Scriptures. ... I am a most unworthy sinner, but I have cried out to the Lord for grace and mercy, and they have covered me completely. ... For the execution to the Indies, I did not make use of intelligence, mathematics or maps. It is simply the fulfillment of what Isaiah had prophesied... No one should fear to undertake any task in the name of our Savior, if it is just and if the intention is purely for his Holy service."

ILLUSTRATION NUMBER TWO

The Church of England was established by Henry VIII in 1534 when the Pope refused to grant him a divorce from Catherine of Aragon. When it became the official state church, the people were placed under the authority of Anglican bishops, who began to lord it over their congregations, acting harsh and cruel. By the late 1500s, it was difficult for committed Christians in England to worship and serve God with freedom.

One group of believers moved to Holland for about 12 years, but found there a hard and difficult life. The Lord used these circumstances to encourage them to explore the possibility of sailing to the New World.

Their search for transportation and a means to send their supplies led them to a group of businessmen who owned merchant ships. Soon 102 passengers set sail for America on a cargo ship named the *Mayflower*. We call them "Pilgrims" in reference to their pilgrimage to a foreign land.

The ship was not designed to carry passengers, so living conditions were miserable. The food consisted of salted beef, pork or fish and hard biscuits. Sanitary facilities were non-existent. The passengers wore the same clothes for the entire voyage. Sleeping quarters were on the wet floor below the main deck, and many on board became deathly ill. The Pilgrims knew it was only by God's mercy that any of them survived.

On the morning of November 9, 1620, sixty-six days after setting sail, the *Mayflower* reached the sandy beaches of Cape Cod in what today is Massachusetts. Though they were in a strange land, with no friends to greet them and no homes or existing towns, the Pilgrims had been obedient to God's call and could at last pray and worship now with complete freedom.

There were many trials, however, in building this first Christian settlement in America. The Pilgrims had to contend with a harsh winter, lack of food, sickness, loneliness and conflicts with the Indians. By spring, half of the group had died. It was primarily their faith in Jesus Christ that gave them the courage to carry on.

A friendly Indian named Squanto, who had learned the English language, taught them how to plant crops. The Pilgrims believed he had been sent to them by the Lord. Because of his advice their gardens flourished. Along with wild game that was available, they now had plenty to eat. In the autumn of 1621, nearly a year after their arrival, the Pilgrims decided to set aside a special time to give thanks to God for His faithfulness. It is a commemoration we still celebrate annually—Thanksgiving.

ILLUSTRATION NUMBER THREE

While the Pilgrims were establishing the first Christian settlement at Plymouth, Puritans still living in England continued to come under mounting persecution. Like the Pilgrims they saw an alternative in America. In the year 1628 a massive exodus began. This migration lasted for about 16 years, during which more than 20,000 Puritans packed up and sailed to America.

The Puritans, above all others, laid America's foundation as a Christian nation. Recognizing the reality of their own sinful natures, they acknowledged the harm that sin caused in their relationship with both Jesus and one another. This willingness to submit to the Lord produced not only a compassion for one another, but a remarkable maturity in the handling of spiritual matters.

The Puritans also strongly emphasized parental responsibility, accountability and authority in the home. They believed it was their God-given responsibility to protect their children and raise them in the ways of the Lord. The Bible was their guide. Christian love and caring for the souls of others characterized the lives of these forefathers. As one of the Puritan leaders, Cotton Mather, wrote, *"Well-ordered families naturally produce a good order in society."*

> THE PURITANS
> LAID AMERICA'S
> FOUNDATION AS
> A CHRISTIAN NATION.

The main reason many today do not know the Puritans' story is the revisionist history that began in the last century. Few negative comments about Puritans can be found in earlier books; historians credited the Puritans with setting the course of this nation. Satan has tried to eradicate the true picture of their critical role in our country. Since rebellion is Satan's specialty, it's no wonder the Puritans have received bad press in recent decades.

ILLUSTRATION NUMBER FOUR

Faith is not inherited. It is not automatically passed on to children and grandchildren. This unfortunate truth is seen repeatedly in the Old Testament in the history of the Israelites. Later generations of Puritans also fell away from the faith of their fathers. These newcomers had not forsaken their homes and followed the Lord's leading to a new land. Instead, they enjoyed the fruit of the blessings the Lord poured out on their predecessors. Though they still attended church, their hearts and minds were more fixed on worldly matters. This growing lack of interest in their spiritual commitment brought the Great Awakening, another intervention by God in the 1730s and '40s.

The first glimmer of light that dawned on this state of spiritual apathy shone in 1734 in Northampton, Massachusetts. Jonathan Edwards was a pastor there who was preaching with God's anointing. It soon became obvious that the Spirit of God was also sweeping over others who preached the Word with a tremendous anointing. Among these were George Whitefield, John Wesley and David Brainerd. As men like these opened God's Word, literally thousands came to know Jesus as their Savior and Lord. People were in awe as the power of God fell on one town after another.

Riding the main roads and through the backwoods on horseback, these ministers traveled hundreds of miles. It is reported that George Whitefield preached more than 18,000 sermons between 1736 and 1770. Through men like this, God was preparing America to become a great nation. The principles on which she would be founded were being established through the preaching of the Word. The spiritual health of her people was being formulated to meet the special calling God had in mind. I believe our unique role was to be a part of God's mission of being the "salt of the earth" and the "light of the world" in these last days. America was being prepared to become a geographical nerve center from which God would take the Gospel of Jesus throughout the world.

Historians also agree that it was the powerful preaching during the Great Awakening that set the tone for the American Revolution and later for our Constitu-

> AMERICA WAS FOUNDED THROUGH THE PREACHING OF THE WORD.

tion. Although our government was designed to be secular—a government of all—Christians were deeply involved in forming our Constitution, our Bill of Rights, and numerous other aspects of our republic form of government. They often led the way in the thinking process. These believers knew the importance of their freedom in Christ and recognized that they could never again submit to a yoke of slavery.

Our Founding Fathers protested for 11 years before they wrote the Declaration of Independence, which listed 27 violations of biblical principles among their complaints against King George III of England.

This document concludes with the statement, *"We ... pledge our lives, our fortunes, and our sacred honor."* Fifty-three of the 56 signers of the Declaration confessed a personal relationship with Jesus Christ. Twenty-four of these men were lawyers and jurists, eleven were merchants, and nine were farmers and large-plantation owners. These educated men of means put their signatures on this Declaration knowing full well that the penalty of death would be theirs if the British caught them.

Five of the signers were captured and tortured as traitors before they died. Twelve had their homes ransacked and burned. Seven lost sons. Nine fought and died from wounds or hardships of the Revolutionary War. Ten had all of their property seized. Some lost a wife through death, and several ended up bankrupt. These men and their families suffered heavy persecution for signing this bill. Yet they were willing to risk everything for a freedom they rightly believed came only from God. Interestingly, a majority of the militia units in the Revolutionary War were composed of a pastor and men from his congregation.

In George Washington's first address to his troops he stated: *"The time is now at hand which must probably determine whether Americans are to be free men or slaves ... consigned to a state of wretchedness from which no human efforts will deliver them. The fate of unborn millions will now depend, under God, on the courage of this Army. Our cruel and unrelenting enemy leaves us on the choice of brave resistance or the most abject submission. We have therefore to resolve to conquer or die."*

John Adams, one of our Founding Fathers and the second president, said, *"Our Constitution was made only for a moral and a religious people. It is wholly inadequate to the government of any other."* His son, John Quincy Adams, the sixth president, stated, *"The highest glory of the American Revolution was this: It connected in one indissoluble bond, the principles of civil government with those of Christianity."*

ILLUSTRATION NUMBER FIVE

After the victory in the Revolutionary War and the framing and adoption of our Constitution, which was put into effect March 4, 1789, the next major move of God was in the establishment of thousands of churches during the 1800s and 1900s. The revivals that started during the Great Awakening in the 1700s continued in the 1800s. Even during the Civil War, God worked in powerful ways among the soldiers on both sides. William Bennett, a minister and Confederate chaplain, wrote in his account *The Great Revival in the Southern Armies*:

In the midst of all the privations and horrors of war "the grace of God appeared" unto thousands and tens of thousands in the camp and in the hospital, "teaching them that, denying ungodliness and worldly lusts, they should live soberly, righteously, and godly in this present world." The subjects of this revival were found among all classes in the army. Generals in high command, and officers of all lower grades, as well as private soldiers, bowed before the Lord of Hosts, and with deep penitence and earnest prayer sought the pardon of sins through the atoning blood of Christ.

> OUR HISTORY CANNOT BE FULLY TOLD WITHOUT OUR SPIRITUAL HERITAGE.

The truth is, the history of our nation is one that cannot be fully told without referencing our spiritual heritage. In 1892, in the case of *The Church of the Holy Trinity vs. The United States*, the Supreme Court stated: *"Our laws and institutions must necessarily be based upon and embody the teachings of the Redeemer of mankind. It is impossible that it should be otherwise and in this sense and to this extent our civilization and our institutions are emphatically Christian. This is historically true from the discovery of this continent to the present hour; we find everywhere a clear recognition of the same truth. These and many other matters add a volume of unofficial declarations to the mass of organic utterances that this is a Christian nation."*

Today there are more than 350,000 Christian churches across our land. In fact, you can hear the Gospel preached every hour through every communication means available. Christian men and women from

America have also taken the Gospel of Christ throughout the world and raised up numerous ministries to meet the various needs of people.

Even as God obviously had a hand in America's past, He challenges His Church today to be salt and light in our present troubled society. In Matthew 5:13-14 Jesus makes two of the most penetrating statements about Christians found anywhere in Scripture: **"You are the salt of the earth"** and **"You are the light of the world."** Jesus gave us our perfect mission statement in these two short sentences. They require a lot of courage to live out and are quite demanding. Our Lord is saying that Christians are the only people in this world who can preserve the good (our function as salt) and have the understanding to help in those areas that matter the most (our function as light). What a challenging and fulfilling adventure Christians are to have in this life on Earth.

> JESUS GAVE US OUR PERFECT MISSION STATEMENT IN THESE TWO SHORT SENTENCES.

SALT

For Jesus to use the word **salt** to describe one of the key functions in the life of a Christian is amazing. Only the wisdom of God could have known what we do today about salt. It is one of the most stable compounds on Earth. On its own, it will not lose its saltiness. Salt becomes ineffective only when it becomes contaminated. This occurs if it is mixed or diluted with some other material or chemical.

To not lose its effectiveness, salt has to remain essentially different from the medium in which it is placed. When kept in a pure condition, it only takes a small amount of salt to accomplish the purpose of adding flavor or acting as a preservative. If God's people remain in a pure state, it will only take a few of us to make a major difference. History records this happening in the first century during the beginning of the church.

"But if the salt loses its saltiness, how can it be made salty again? It is no longer good for anything" (Matthew 5:13). There is a principle of life that Jesus is teaching here. If Christians assimilate something other than the purity of God's Word, we face a great danger of becoming contaminated. Our influence in this world will only happen if we are distinctively different. **"What does a believer have in common with an unbeliever? What agreement is there between the temple of God and idols? For we are the temple of the living God. As God has said: 'I will live with them and walk among them, and I will be their God, and they will be my people.' 'Therefore come out from them and separate, says the Lord. Touch no unclean thing, and I will receive you'"** (2 Corinthians 6:15-17).

Mixing the standards of the world with God's standards is one of the major temptations the enemy is using today. It causes Christians to become contaminated and lose their "saltiness." It is vital to our mission that we understand what being **"the salt of the earth"** entails. We must be a preserver of the good.

LIGHT

Jesus then proclaimed that Christians are **"the light of the world."** The world is in a state of darkness, even though its people are always talking about their enlightenment. There are many Scriptures that confirm this truth. **"For he has rescued us from the dominion of darkness and brought us into the kingdom of the Son he loves"** (Colossians 1:13). **"For you were once darkness, but now you are light in the Lord"** (Ephesians 5:8). **"But you are a chosen people ... a people belonging to God ... who called you out of darkness into his wonderful light"** (1 Peter 2:9). Only Christians have been brought into the light; the people of the world remain in spiritual darkness.

The world does not recognize its darkness, however. One of the catchphrases of the Renaissance in the 15th and 16th centuries was that "knowledge brings light." Many replaced God's knowledge with man's reasoning, placing human insight above God's revealed wisdom. They replaced the worship of God with the worship of man's intellect.

Mankind does not realize that our knowledge has only increased our understanding of *things*—science, biology, commerce, pleasure, etc.—not the *real factors* that are critical to the makeup of a successful and peaceful life. This is why the world's vast accumulation of knowledge has only brought us to the many predicaments we see around us. We humans have failed in the most important area of all. <u>We do not know what to do with our knowledge.</u> Look at the failed relationships between people and nations. We don't seem to understand that **knowledge only gives us the ability to analyze. It does <u>not</u> give us wisdom, therefore, the answers as to what to do.** Jesus taught that Christians should give off this light that the world so desperately needs.

JESUS ALONE IS THE LIGHT OF THE WORLD.

The world does not have light because Jesus alone is the light of the world: **"'I am the light of the world. Whoever follows me will never walk in darkness, but will have the light of life'"** (John 8:12). Only Christians can reflect the light and life of the Son of God. When a person is born again into His spiritual Kingdom, the Spirit of Jesus Christ begins to live in and through that individual. **"Don't you know that you yourselves are God's temple and that God's Spirit lives in you?"** (1 Corinthians 3:16).

Christians are not the light of the world because of who we are, but because we reflect the nature and character of Him who now lives in us by His Spirit. Jesus said, **"This is the verdict: light** [meaning Himself] **has come into the world, but men loved darkness instead of light because their deeds were evil. Everyone who does evil hates the light, and will not come into the light for fear that his deeds will be exposed. But whoever lives by the truth comes into the light, so that it may be seen plainly that what he has done has been done through God"** (John 3:19-21).

As the light of Jesus Christ shines through us, it exposes the error of man's way of thinking. That is why the Pharisees and scribes, who supposedly had all the answers, hated Jesus so much. It is why the people of the world today, who still think they have the answers, hate many of the teachings found in Scripture. Such a light exposes the sins of mankind that they do not want revealed.

OUR PERFECT EXAMPLE

Salt describes our state of being, and **light** describes our state of doing. Jesus Himself was our perfect example of these two words that describe our mission. He did not have the attributes most people would consider necessary to accomplish great things. We've all read about how He lived in poverty and was reared in obscurity. He never received a formal education, never possessed wealth and never traveled extensively. Yet in just three and a half years of ministry the effects of His life on mankind were greater than that of anyone else in history.

The names of great statesmen come and go. Philosophers, scientists and theologians are soon forgotten. But the name of this man Jesus shines forth more and more. Once each week the wheels of commerce cease their turning, as multitudes gather to pay homage to Him. He was God on Earth in the form of a human being. He truly proved that it only takes a small amount of light to make a major difference in a dark world. And the same Spirit that lived in Him lives in all Christians who have truly been born again.

It is every Christian's duty to be His ambassador by fulfilling God's mission to be **the salt of the earth** and **the light of the world**. However, according to Bible prophecy, there will be tremendous spiritual warfare carried on by the enemy in the last days of the Church Age. God has given us Scriptures about the future so we will have insight about how the enemy will carry out this spiritual warfare. As we travel through this book the enemy's tactics will be clearly exposed. That way we can prepare ourselves to overcome his schemes.

MANKIND LOVES DARKNESS

Since the Fall, man has loved darkness rather than light. He likes it this way! It is his nature. The trouble with mankind is not one of intellect; the Bible tells us it is our sinful nature, sin is integral to who we are (see Romans 5:12 and 7:14-25). In its fallen, sinful state the world can be a rotten, foul, polluted place. Left alone, it would probably self-destruct. It needs a preservative and a light that shines brightly, showing forth the love of God. Jesus stated that Christians, and Christians alone, are that preservative and that source of illumination. No one else is capable of fulfilling these two functions regardless of how educated they may be, or how hard they try.

The only way this dark world will find the answers it seeks is from the life and teachings of Jesus Christ! Only Christians are **"the light of the world."** The truth of this statement is why Jesus tells us that our light <u>must</u> shine before men, that they may see our good deeds. **"Let your light shine before men, that they may see your good deeds and praise your Father in heaven"** (Matthew 5:16).

In bringing up the biblical truth that knowledge and education are <u>not</u> the answer to mankind's problems, I am not suggesting that I don't support education. Quite the contrary! I have a college degree, and our own three children and the six we took into our home to raise all went to college. Eight of the nine received their college degrees, and three earned a master's. My wife and I founded what is now one of the major Christian schools in Phoenix. I served as president of this school for 17 years and was on the board of Phoenix Christian High School for ten years. There is no question that education is important. But Scripture makes clear that it is the Spirit of God and the Word of God that enlightens mankind with the wisdom we need to understand and apply what knowledge we have.

FULFILLMENT OF OUR MISSION

To be the **salt of the earth** and the **light of the world** is an exciting challenge, but it does not happen just because the words are spoken.

There must be a continued audit of the fruit of any mission statement; otherwise, how can you know if it is being fulfilled?

In these last days, we are living in one of the toughest times ever to be salt and light—especially in America! There has never been a society with as much power to teach its standards as the American society now has. That is one of the reasons why God warns us often about the ways of the world. The world is the enemy's main attack vehicle to pollute the purity of Christians, thereby weakening our ability to function as salt and light. **"You adulterous people, don't you know that friendship with the world is hatred toward God? Anyone who chooses to be a friend of the world becomes an enemy of God"** (James 4:4). **"Do not love the world or anything in the world. If anyone loves the world, the love of the Father is not in him. For everything in the world— the cravings of sinful man, the lust of his eyes and the boasting of what he has and does—comes not from the Father but from the world"** (1 John 2:15-16).

> WE ARE LIVING IN ONE OF THE TOUGHEST TIMES EVER TO BE SALT AND LIGHT.

God warns us that the systems developed by mankind are controlled by our spiritual enemy. He uses them as a means to wage war against Christians. We are told in Scripture that we are to live <u>in</u> the world, but not to be <u>of</u> the world. This is because spiritually we are no longer citizens of the kingdom of this world, but have become citizens of the Kingdom of God. The Apostle Paul considered this world dead to him and himself dead to this world. He said, **"May I never boast except in the cross of our Lord Jesus Christ, through which the world has been crucified to me, and I to the world"** (Galatians 6:14).

When we bow to Jesus Christ as our personal Savior and Lord, we experience a spiritual rebirth by the power of the Holy Spirit. From that point on, we are no longer a part of the world's spiritual family. Colossians 1:13 states, **"For He has rescued us out of the darkness**

and gloom of Satan's kingdom and brought us into the kingdom of His dear Son" (The Living Bible). Satan's objective is to prevent us from carrying out God's mission to function as salt and light. Satan uses his kingdom—the world, or society—as one of his key attack vehicles to contaminate our being salt and to dim our light. However, all Christians are equipped with a power greater than the influence of Satan's world system so we might fulfill our mission. **"You, dear children, are from God and have overcome them, because the one who is in you** [the Holy Spirit—God Himself] **is greater than the one who is in the world** [Satan]" (1 John 4:4).

As we look at the prophetic Scriptures that reveal the tactics Satan is using against America, we will see how he is trying in these last days to destroy God's special call for Christians. In this last generation his methods have been highly successful. We have not preserved the godly standards that the majority of people in our society lived by since the founding of our country.

Before we discuss these prophetic passages, however, it is important that we review some of the fundamental characteristics that make up the Kingdom of God and the kingdom of the world. Our understanding of the differences between these two is important before looking at any Scriptures about the last days.

QUESTIONS FOR GROUP DISCUSSION AND/OR TO BE ANSWERED INDIVIDUALLY

What effect do you think Christianity had on the way America was founded?

_____

_____

_____

_____

_____

_____

In what ways will the influence of the Church be as powerful in 21st-century America as it was in the 18th, 19th and 20th centuries? Give reasons for your response.

_____

_____

_____

_____

_____

In what special ways has the American church fulfilled the role of salt and light in society? Where have we fallen short?

_____

_____

_____

_____

_____

_____

Have you fulfilled your "mission statement" of being salt and light? What practical ways can we maintain our saltiness and shed more light? Explain.

_____

_____

_____

_____

_____

_____

_____

What does Scripture mean when it says "that we are to live in the world, but not to be of the world"?

_____

_____

_____

_____

_____

_____

_____

As you begin the study of *You Are Salt and Light*, what are some of your initial impressions?

_____

_____

_____

_____

_____

_____

_____

CHAPTER TWO

THE LAST DAYS
OF THE CHURCH AGE

Many thoughtful Christians believe we are in the last days of the Church Age. There are biblical reasons why this is widely felt. I want to discuss a few of them, because we need to realize that <u>according to Scripture we could be living in the most critical and deceptive time of spiritual warfare the church has ever encountered.</u>

THE AGES OF TIME

It can be determined from the Bible that the time span from our early ancestors to when God called Abraham was around 2000 years. From Abraham, which was the beginning of the Jewish Nation, to the start of the Church Age and the time of the Gentiles, was also about 2000 years. And from the beginning of the Church Age to the present has been roughly 2000 years. I feel this is significant.

It's as though God has dealt with mankind in three distinct periods of time, each about 2000 years long. Throughout Scripture, the number three denotes divine perfection. For example, the Trinity: the Father, Son and Holy Spirit. Another illustration is the fact that the universe is made up of three distinct

> GOD HAS DEALT WITH MANKIND IN THREE DISTINCT PERIODS OF TIME.

things: space, time and matter. Even these can be broken down into three different parts. Space is length, depth and height. Time is past, present and future. Matter is solid, liquid or gas.

We know little about the first 2000 years. All God chose to tell us is found in the first eleven chapters of the Bible. During this time He dealt with mankind through select individuals. Scholars often refer to this period as the Patriarchal Dispensation, because it includes the extremely early fathers of the human race, including Adam, Noah and everyone prior to the time of Abraham.

The second 2000 years began with the call of Abraham in Genesis 12 and covers the remainder of the Old Testament. Here God shifts His emphasis from the history of mankind in general to the life of a single individual and his descendants, who become the Jewish race. Through this line God's Son would eventually be born. This second period is called the Jewish Dispensation, because God's dealings with mankind were focused on one nationality. **"The Lord had said to Abram, "Leave your country, your people and your father's household and go to the land I will show you. I will make you into a great nation and I will bless you; I will make your name great, and you will be a blessing. I will bless those who bless you, and whoever curses you I will curse; and all peoples on earth will be blessed through you"** (Genesis 12:1-3).

> EVERY CHRISTIAN BECOMES A TEMPLE OF THE HOLY SPIRIT.

The third way God has dealt with mankind changed with the death and resurrection of Jesus. This was the beginning of the Church Age, during which time God began to deal personally with each individual. He does this by taking up residence in each person through the Holy Spirit. This happens when they accept Jesus Christ as Lord and Savior. Every person who becomes a Christian is spiritually born again into the Kingdom of God and becomes a temple of the Holy Spirit. **"Don't you know that you yourselves are God's temple and that**

God's Spirit lives in you?" (1 Corinthians 3:16). This uniquely differs from how God dealt with mankind in the previous 4000 years. This last 2000-year period is also called the Spiritual Dispensation, because all who become Christians receive the Holy Spirit. In this time period, God also deals primarily with the Gentiles.

The history of these three distinct periods is one of the reasons I feel we are living in the last days of the Church Age. This era is now approaching 2000 years—the same amount of time the other two periods lasted. As it comes to a close, we do not want to be like the Jewish people, who did not recognize the prophetic events God had foretold. We need to study the biblical prophesies about the end of our dispensation. This is critical to an understanding of Satan's intense spiritual opposition against the church in America.

THE SIGNIFICANCE OF 6000 YEARS

Six is a significant number in the Bible. It is associated with human beings and their labor. Man was created on the sixth day; he was commanded to work for six days and rest on the seventh; he was to work the ground for six years and then let it rest in the seventh. Revelation 13:18 says that the number of man is 666, which is commonly referred to as the mark of the beast. Six signifies "secular completeness."

The biblical account of human beings has now spanned nearly 6000 years. There is still one more period of time that God will deal with mankind. It will be quite different from the other three. That last period is called the millennium, and Revelation seems to indicate it will last for 1000 years. It will begin at the end of this current Church Age. No longer will mankind run the affairs on Earth; instead, Christ will rule in peace. Before this happens, there is still much to take place in the remaining years of the Church Age—however many that may be. One of the reasons why the Body of Christ has suffered so many spiritual defeats in recent years is that we lack an understanding of many of these prophetic Scriptures about the last days. In the words of the prophet Hosea: **"My people are destroyed** [defeated or overcome] **from lack of knowledge"** (Hosea 4:6).

THE SIGNIFICANCE OF 7000 YEARS

The 1000 years of Christ's millennial reign plus the 6000 years that mankind has run the Earth totals 7000 years. Throughout Scripture the <u>number seven denotes completeness</u>. For example, it took seven days for God to complete His creation. On the seventh day He rested, which is one indication why the last 1000-year period of mankind on Earth will be one of peace and rest. There are many questions about this final 1000-year period, but just like those who lived in previous eras, mankind has never been given complete insight into how God will work in future periods of time.

RETURN OF THE JEWS TO PALESTINE: A MAJOR PROPHETIC SIGN

The return of the Jewish people to Palestine and the development of their nation, after 1900 years of dispersion throughout the world, is considered by many to be the greatest fulfillment of Bible prophecy, apart from those surrounding the life of Jesus. Both Testaments speak of this prophetic sign. Nearly 2000 years ago Jesus stated that Jerusalem would be trampled down by the Gentiles until the end of this Church Age. From A.D. 70 to 1967, the city of Jerusalem was under the control of other nations. The restoration of Israel as a nation in 1948 also serves as a major prophetic sign that we are living in the last days of the Church Age.

THE RESTORATION OF ISRAEL SERVES AS A MAJOR PROPHETIC SIGN.

Because the Jews rejected their Messiah, in A.D. 70, God allowed the Roman army to swoop down on Jerusalem and destroy both the city and their temple. The Jews were then scattered to more than 100 countries for nearly 1900 years. But God remained faithful to His Word. He kept His promise to Abraham and protected his descendants, their nationality and their heritage. We have full evidence of this today. The Jews are the only people in history to be without a country for that long and still keep their identity.

From A.D. 70 to 614 the Romans ruled Palestine. Then the Persians conquered it and ruled until about A.D. 700, when Islam spread from Spain to India. Except for brief periods during the Crusades of the Dark Ages, the Arabs were in control. From A.D. 1500 to 1800 Palestine fell into disuse. There were only 1500 Jews in the entire land.

During the 1800s the Jewish population began to slowly increase. By 1865, Jerusalem had a population of 18,000, with about half of the inhabitants being Jewish. In the late 1800s, the Jewish people began to suffer persecution in many of the lands where they had been living. God used these hardships to cause them to start thinking about returning to their homeland. This dream was intensified through the distribution of a pamphlet called *The Jewish State*, written by Theodor Herzl in 1897.

By 1914 there were 90,000 Jews in Palestine. God was moving to bring about the second restoration of Abraham's descendants, just as the Old Testament prophets had written.

The next major event occurred in November of 1917 when English statesman Arthur Balfour wrote the Jewish Federation stating that his country would make a declaration to help the Jewish people return to Palestine. England fulfilled that commitment after World War I when they gained control of Palestine from the Turkish government.

England's pledge to help the Jewish people owed much to a Jewish scientist named Chaim Weizmann. The August 1982 issue of *Gospel Truth* magazine reported:

Weizmann was a brilliant research chemist, and became the first president of the modern state of Israel. However, he was born in Russian Poland. He lectured in the University of Geneva in biochemistry, and in 1904 at Manchester, England. The thrilling thing in this romantic story is that when World War I broke out in 1914, God had raised up Weizmann in Poland, brought him over to England, and when it looked as though Britain might not be able to terminate the war victoriously, Weizmann worked in the British laboratories from 1916 to 1918 on acetone—a color-less, flammable, volatile liquid. In that capacity, he performed a notable service for the British government during the latter years of World War I by discovering and developing a method for synthesizing acetone (a substance essential to the manufacture of a smokeless powder called cordite). The discovery of this secret gave him national recognition. In 1917 Prime Minister David Lloyd George offered him a reward for this spectacular achievement. Weizmann chose that the British government provide a national, geographical home for the Jewish people. In November, 1917, Britain issued the celebrated Balfour Declaration in which it formally announced its favorable attitude towards the establishment in Palestine of a national home for Jews.

ABRAHAM'S DESCENDANTS ONCE AGAIN POSSESSED THE PROMISED LAND.

The next 30 years saw the Jewish population in Israel mushroom to 710,000. It appears God used the same method to detach the Jewish people from their homes among the Gentile nations that He used to wean them from Egypt back in the days of Moses. In Egypt, it was persecution from the hands of Pharaoh. In the 1920s, '30s and early '40s it was persecution from Nazi Germany and the Communist government in Russia.

It was 30 years to the month from the Balfour Declaration that a United Nations mandate returned part of the land of Palestine to the Jewish people, in November 1947. I don't believe this period of 30 years was just happenstance. Thirty years has always denoted maturity in God's dealings with the Jewish people. There are examples of this in Scripture—the most significant being that Jesus was 30 years old when He began His ministry. Another is David, who became king when he was 30.

On May 14, 1948 the U.N.-issued mandate became effective, and Abraham's descendants once again possessed the Promised Land. This restoration is one of the great fulfillments of prophecy. Several Old Testament writers mention this second restoration of the Jews to Palestine. **"In that day the Lord will reach out his hand <u>a second time</u> to reclaim the remnant that is left of his people from Assyria, from Lower Egypt, from Upper Egypt, from Cush, from Elam, from Babylonia, from Hamath and from the islands of the sea** [here "islands of the sea" means "many nations"]. **He will raise a banner for the nations and gather the exiles of Israel; he will assemble the scattered people of Judah from the four quarters of the earth"** (Isaiah 11:11-12). By the words of Isaiah we can know that God is <u>not</u> referring to the first restoration of the Jews to Palestine, which was from their 70 years of captivity by the Babylonian Empire. Not only does Isaiah specifically say the <u>second</u> restoration, he also mentions the Israelites returning from many nations, which was <u>not</u> the case when they returned from Babylon.

Similarly, both Jeremiah and Ezekiel prophesied of the second restoration by referring to the Jews returning from many countries and nations. **"'However, the days are coming,' declares the Lord, 'when man will no longer say,** *as surely as the Lord lives, who brought the Israelites up out of Egypt,* **but they will say,** *as surely as the Lord lives who brought the Israelites up out of the land of the north and out of the countries where he had banished them.* **For I will restore them to the land I gave their forefathers'"** (Jeremiah 16:14-15). **"'Therefore say:** *This is what the Sovereign Lord says: Although I sent them far away among the nations and scattered them among the countries, yet for a little while I have been a sanctuary for them in the countries where they have gone.* **Therefore say:** *This is what the Sovereign Lord says: I will gather you from the nations and bring you back from the countries where you have been scattered, and I will give you back the land of Israel again'"** (Ezekiel 11:16-17).

This same prophet also made one of the best-known prophecies about the second return of the Jewish people to the land promised to

Abraham in Ezekiel 37:1-12. **"The hand of the Lord was upon me, and he brought me out by the Spirit of the Lord and set me in the middle of a valley; it was full of bones. He led me back and forth among them, and I saw a great many bones on the floor of the valley, bones that were very dry. He asked me, 'Son of man, can these bones live?' I said, 'O Sovereign Lord, you alone know.'"** The dry bones Ezekiel saw represented the Jewish people. They were like the dead, since they were not fulfilling their purpose as Abraham's descendants, because they had been scattered throughout the Earth.

Ezekiel continues: **"Then he said to me, 'Prophesy to these bones and say to them, *Dry bones, hear the word of the Lord!* This is what the Sovereign Lord says to these bones: *I will make breath enter you, and you will come to life. I will attach tendons to you and make flesh come upon you and cover you with skin; I will put breath in you, and you will come to life. Then you will know that I am the Lord.'*

So I prophesied as I was commanded. And, as I was prophesying there was a noise, a rattling sound, and the bones came together, bone to bone. I looked, and tendons and flesh appeared on them and skin covered them, but there was no breath in them."**

Through the message of Herzl's book and England's Balfour Declaration, the Jewish people began to return to Israel en masse ... taking the form of a nation once again.

"Then he said to me, 'Prophesy to the breath; prophesy, son of man, and say to it, *This is what the Sovereign Lord says: Come from the four winds, O breath and breathe into these slain, that they may live.'* So I prophesied as he commanded me, and breath entered them; they came to life and stood up on their feet—a vast army." On May 14, 1948 the Jewish people once again came to life as a nation as the mandate issued by the United Nations became effective.

"Then he said to me: 'Son of man, these bones are the whole house of Israel. They say, *Our bones are dried up and our hope is gone; we are cut off.* Therefore, prophesy and say to them: *This is what the Sovereign Lord says: O my people, I am going to open your*

graves and bring you up from them; I will bring you back to the land of Israel'" (Ezekiel 37:1-12). **"This is what the Sovereign Lord says:** *'I will take the Israelites out of the nations where they have gone. I will gather them from all around and bring them back into their own land. I will make them one nation in the land, on the mountain of Israel'"* (Ezekiel 37:21-22).

ON MAY 14, 1948
THE JEWISH PEOPLE
CAME TO LIFE
AS A NATION

For centuries, the Lord seemed to hide His face from Abraham's descendants. But God's faithfulness prevailed. Because of the promise He made to Abraham, God kept His covenant. The land of Israel is again the home of the patriarch's descendants. The nation is alive once more! The fulfillment of the prophecies found in the Old Testament is now recorded in our history books.

BATTLING FOR THEIR HOMELAND

Several wars have taken place since the Jewish control of the land. The surrounding Arab nations have repeatedly tried to destroy them. Studying the way the Jewish people won those wars, even though the odds were greatly against them, is like reading of the miraculous victories in the days of Joshua in the Old Testament. Within hours of the declaration of the Jewish state, Arab forces began dropping bombs to rid the land of its 710,000 Jews. God had different plans, though, and the Israelites gained the upper hand in this first conflict. An armistice followed, even though the Arabs still had control of the old city of Jerusalem and the remains of the temple wall.

The next conflict occurred in 1956, when President Gamal Abdel Nasser of Egypt called for a holy war. The Egyptian army, equipped with Soviet weapons, moved into the Sinai and began a second round of fighting. However, this conflict was again brief, with the Israelites teaching the Arabs a dramatic lesson.

By 1958, only ten years after the establishment of the new Jewish state, major progress had been made in several areas: The Jewish population had risen to 1.8 million. Most people were employed and self-sufficient. Agricultural productivity was up 600%. To house the growing population, 150,000 new dwellings had been completed. Other areas of progress included: national insurance, several welfare and health services, roads, water, electricity, sanitary facilities, irrigation and participation in free elections.

ON JUNE 7, ISRAEL GAINED POSSESSION OF THE OLD CITY.

A third conflict broke out in 1967 as Arab resentment again exploded, beginning what has come to be known as the Six-Day War. The Arabs launched an all-out attack, but Israel retaliated with lightning speed and again soundly defeated them. The war started on June 4. The next day, Israel bombed the airfields of Egypt, Syria, Jordan and Iraq, destroying 452 planes in three hours. That same day, their ground forces moved against the Egyptians at four different points in the Sinai.

On June 6, Israel counterattacked against Jordanian troops in Jerusalem and took everything except the old city. On June 7, Israel gained possession of the old city for the first time since A.D. 70. A quarter of a million Jews headed for the Wailing Wall. The site where Solomon built the temple for the Lord was back in Jewish hands! On June 9, Israel drove the Syrians from the Golan Heights, penetrated the Sinai to the Suez Canal and took the Gaza Strip. On June 10 all parties agreed to a ceasefire.

The fourth conflict began on October 6, 1973, which was Yom Kippur, the most holy day of the year for the Jews—their Day of Atonement. It looked bad at first. In the south, Egyptian aircraft and artillery bombarded the Sinai, and 70,000 of their troops and 1,000 tanks crossed the Suez Canal. In the north, 40,000 Syrian troops with 800 tanks attacked the Golan Heights. Within a few days Israel stopped all advances on both fronts and began to penetrate enemy lines with amazing speed, moving to within 62 miles of Cairo. The Arab nations again faced defeat, and on October 25, 1973, just 20 days from the war's beginning, a ceasefire was proclaimed.

Another conflict began on June 6, 1982, when the State of Israel launched a massive thrust into Lebanon aimed at removing PLO (Palestine Liberation Organization) terrorist gunners from their northern border. During this brief encounter, 86 Soviet-built MiG fighters were shot down by the Israeli air force without a single loss of their own. *Business Week*, September 20, 1982 reported: *"The latest air war was lopsided, too, but this time in Israel's favor. When Syria sent up 60 Soviet-built MiG fighters to defend its SAM batteries, 90 U.S.-made Israelite jets pounced on and shot down 36 MiGs without a single loss. On the following day, Syria dispatched 50 more MiGs to challenge the Israeli air force—and not one of those jets returned to base, the Israelis claim."*

The purpose of this brief review is to help you understand that we are living in the last days of the Christian dispensation. Sometimes we fail to remember the important role the Jewish people have played in God's plan for mankind. Because of God's faithfulness in keeping His promise to Abraham, the Jewish people have been a tremendous blessing. They gave us the Scriptures. The majority of God's Word centers on the history of the Jewish people. They are the race God chose for Jesus to be born into as He came to Earth in the form of man. They began the early church.

Describing events to come after their second restoration, Ezekiel writes: **"My servant David** [Jesus'] **will be king over them, and they will all have one shepherd. They will follow my laws and be careful to keep my decrees** [we know this has not yet happened]**. They will live in the land I gave to my servant Jacob** [remember, he was the father of the 12 sons who formed the twelve tribes of Israel]**, the land where your fathers lived. ... I will make a covenant of peace with them; it will be an everlasting covenant. I will establish them and increase their numbers, and I will put my sanctuary among**

them forever. My dwelling place will be with them; I will be their God, and they will be my people. Then the nations will know that I, the Lord, make Israel holy, when my sanctuary is among them forever" (Ezekiel 37:24-28).

The Jewish people will someday acknowledge and accept Jesus, as foretold by Zechariah, another Old Testament prophet. **"On that day, when all the nations of the earth are gathered against her, I will make Jerusalem an immovable rock for all the nations ... on that day I will set out to destroy all the nations that attack Jerusalem. And I will pour out on the house of David and the inhabitants of Jerusalem a spirit of grace and supplication. They will look on me, the one they have pierced** [what they did to Jesus at the Crucifixion] **and mourn for him as one grieves for a firstborn son"** (Zechariah 12:3, 9-10).

> GOD ALSO RECORDED SOME CRUCIAL PROPHECIES FOR CHRISTIANS.

There can be no doubt as to the prophetic times in which we live, but the main message of this book is not merely to review God's timetable. We cannot just be detached observers as the Jewish people fulfill end-times Scriptures. God also recorded some crucial prophecies for Christians regarding this same period. These were given to guide us spiritually so that in these troubled times we might prepare ourselves to fulfill our mission to be the "salt of the earth" and the "light of the world."

The days in which we are living imply that something of an evil or disaster nature is about to happen. A part of what I feel is that it will be something momentous ... frighteningly big in fact that could produce amazement and wonder. Anyway, let me make clear that the fateful days in which we live demand vigilance on the part of God's people. We certainly need to be awake, alert and watchful. It would be foolish to remain naïve as to what is happening.

Prior to WWII, one could scarcely have imagined there would be a Nuclear Age, a Space Age or a Computer Age. Obviously, all the things taking place at this time are no accident; everything is happening for a purpose. God has not been caught off-guard. He has known all along what would happen, and when and how. That is why He has warned His people through the prophetic Scriptures about the last days. It is especially important for us in America to understand these key Scriptures because we too have been a nation highly favored by God. Due to this undeniable fact, it is easy to understand why Satan's attacks would be the most severe against Christians in our country.

QUESTIONS FOR GROUP DISCUSSION AND/OR TO BE ANSWERED INDIVIDUALLY

What is your emotional response to this chapter? For example, are you frightened, sobered, depressed, excited, expectant, etc.? Why?

_____

_____

_____

_____

_____

_____

With the nation of Israel and its return to the Promised Land, do you place a more serious emphasis on the end times message? Why or why not?

_____

_____

_____

_____

_____

_____

Attempt for a moment to see things from Satan's perspective. What would your feelings be about the Jewish nation? About the United States of America?

_____

_____

_____

_____

_____

_____

Have you been captured yet by Christ's message about His followers being salt and light in the world? Why or why not?

_____

_____

_____

_____

_____

_____

_____

Can you give an example of a way you are demonstrating increased vigilance or watchfulness as a follower of Jesus Christ?

_____

_____

_____

_____

_____

What does being salt and light mean to you? How can we recognize if we are being contaminated?

_____

_____

_____

_____

_____

_____

_____

_____

CHAPTER THREE

WHY YOU MUST BE BORN AGAIN

In a day when the spiritual battle lines are being clearly drawn, it is important to know for sure that you are on the right side. So the next fundamental truth to have a proper grasp of is the relationship between the prophetic warnings about the end-times and what it means to be born again. Personal salvation is the cornerstone of the Christian faith. That's because being born again is a requirement to enter the Kingdom of Heaven. Understanding what it means to be born again also shows us why Christians are the only people who can truly function as the **salt of the earth** and the **light of the world**.

"After dark one night a Jewish religious leader named Nicodemus, a member of the sect of the Pharisees, came for an interview with Jesus. 'Sir,' he said, 'we all know that God has sent You to teach us. Your miracles are proof of this.' Jesus replied, 'With all the earnestness I possess I tell you this: Unless you are born again, you can never get into the Kingdom of God.' 'Born again!' exclaimed Nicodemus. 'What do You mean? How can an old man go back into his mother's womb and be born again?' Jesus replied, 'What I am telling you so earnestly is this: Unless one is born of water [the normal process of physical birth] **and the Spirit** [spiritual rebirth]**, he cannot enter the Kingdom of God. Men can only reproduce human life, but the Holy Spirit gives new life from heaven; so don't be surprised at My statement that you must be born again!'"** (John 3:1-7, The Living Bible)

There are many people today who, like Nicodemus of old, do not understand what it means to be "born again." We live in the physical world; hence, our natural tendency is to think in physical terms. It is difficult for us to think in the spiritual realm, which is necessary to comprehend spiritual truths. But every human being is **primarily a spiritual being**. It is the only part of us that will live forever. The physical is secondary and returns to the elements of the Earth. Physical life is like a vapor compared to our spiritual life, which will last for eternity.

> BUT EVERY HUMAN BEING IS PRIMARILY A SPIRITUAL BEING.

The Bible says that when God created mankind, He **"created man in his own image, in the image of God he created him; male and female he created them"** (Genesis 1:27). God is a spiritual being. Thus, to be created in His image means that mankind was created in God's spiritual image. Our body is made up of the physical elements of this Earth, and that is what it will return to. Its main purpose is to house our spiritual being for the brief time that we live here, preparing for our life hereafter.

Both Paul and Peter referred to our physical body as a tent, something that is temporary. Paul wrote, **"Now we know that if the earthly tent we live in is destroyed, we have a building from God, an eternal house in heaven, not built by human hands"** (2 Corinthians 5:1). **"I think it is right to refresh your memory as long as I live in the tent of this body, because I know that I will soon put it aside, as our Lord Jesus Christ has made clear to me"** (2 Peter 1:13). In Heaven, the mortal body that currently houses our spiritual being will be replaced with an immortal body.

To appreciate the fundamental truth that we must be born again, we also need to understand that there are **two completely different spiritual kingdoms**. Every person belongs to one or the other. We cannot be a member of both at the same time. **I cannot overemphasize this important spiritual truth.** We can belong to the Kingdom of God, also called the Kingdom of Heaven, whose ruler is Jesus Christ. Or we can belong to the kingdom of the world, whose ruler is Satan. To help us comprehend the spiritual warfare that the Bible prophesies for the last days, it is necessary to understand the fundamental differences between these two spiritual domains.

THE TWO SPIRITUAL KINGDOMS

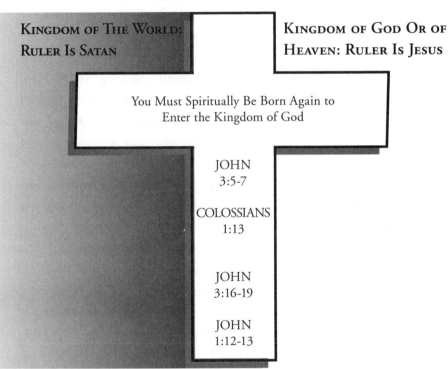

KINGDOM OF THE WORLD: RULER IS SATAN

KINGDOM OF GOD OR OF HEAVEN: RULER IS JESUS

You Must Spiritually Be Born Again to Enter the Kingdom of God

JOHN 3:5-7

COLOSSIANS 1:13

JOHN 3:16-19

JOHN 1:12-13

The phrase **"unless you are born again,"** used by Jesus when speaking to Nicodemus, refers to a spiritual birth, not a physical one. Every baby is born with a physical body, but also as a spiritual being into a spiritual family, or kingdom. The Bible teaches that Adam and Eve's disobedience brought about both physical and spiritual death to all of their descendants. This death can better be understood as separation from God. Therefore, every person is born into this world as members of the kingdom of the world and spiritually separated from God's Kingdom. This is the spiritual condition everyone has inherited from Adam and Eve. **"Therefore, just as sin entered the world through one man** [our forefather Adam], **and death through sin, and this way death** [separation from God] **came to all men, because all sinned"** (Romans 5:12).

> "UNLESS YOU ARE BORN AGAIN" REFERS TO A SPIRITUAL BIRTH, NOT PHYSICAL.

One of the strongest statements regarding this truth actually came from Jesus in His reply to Nicodemus. I will repeat these verses for emphasis, **"What I am telling you so earnestly is this: Unless one is born of water** [physical birth] **and the Spirit** [conceived by the Holy Spirit and reborn spiritually into the Kingdom of God], **he cannot enter the Kingdom of God. Men can only reproduce human life, but the Holy Spirit gives new life from heaven; so don't be surprised at My statement that you must be born again!"** (John 3:5-7, The Living Bible).

So we are born spiritually "on the wrong side of the tracks." We come into this world with a sinful nature and as members of Satan's kingdom. Romans 7 says that it is a spiritual law—we sin because of our heritage. Our natural instinct is to be self-centered. Young children, for example, will naturally lie or cheat, bite, scratch and hit as they look after their own self-interests. Parents do not have to teach them to be this way.

The natural instinct of every person, being a member of the kingdom of the world, is to pursue self-exaltation, self-glorification and self-satisfaction. It was this same self-centered attitude that brought about the fall of Satan. It is why God cast him out of His Kingdom, even though he held a high position. The Bible says of Satan, **"You said in your heart, 'I will ascend to heaven; I will raise my throne above** the stars of God; I will sit enthroned on the mount of assembly, on the utmost heights of the sacred mountain. I will ascend above the tops of the clouds; I will make myself like the Most High'" (Isaiah 14:13-14). Notice the repeated use of the word "I." *I will do this; I will do that.*

Because we are born into the kingdom of the world, we have this same natural instinct. We live to serve ourselves. When we try to decide for ourselves what is right and wrong rather than following the teachings of God, we're effectively aspiring to take the place of God. Examine the nature of Jesus, who walked here on Earth in the fullness of the Holy Spirit. He is the only person conceived by the Spirit of God in a woman's womb and the only one born as a member of the Kingdom of God. He said, **"I tell you the truth, the Son can do nothing by himself; he can do only what he sees his Father doing, because whatever the Father does the Son also does"** (John 5:19). **"By myself I can do nothing; I judge only as I hear, and my judgment is just, for I seek not to please myself but him who sent me"** (John 5:30).

FREEDOM FROM THE KINGDOM OF THE WORLD

We all need to be freed from the spiritual kingdom of the world, which we were born into at birth. The Bible teaches there is only one way this can happen. As Jesus told Nicodemus, we must be born again spiritually. We must be convicted of sin and <u>spiritually</u> born again to enter the spiritual Kingdom of God.

How are we born again? The Word of God states that this spiritual rebirth takes place when we accept Jesus Christ as our Lord and Savior. **"Before anything else existed, there was Christ, with God. He has always been alive and is Himself God. He created everything there is—nothing exists that He didn't make. Eternal life is in Him, and this life gives light to all mankind. ... But although He made the world, the world didn't recognize Him when He came. Even in His own land and among His own people, the Jews, He was not accepted. Only a few would welcome and receive Him. <u>But to all who</u>**

received him, He gave the right to become children of God. All they needed to do was to trust Him to save them. All those who believe this are reborn!—not a physical rebirth resulting from human passion or plan—but from the will of God" (John 1:1-4, 10-13, The Living Bible).

When we are spiritually born again, the Holy Spirit literally takes up residence in our being, just as He is in the being of Jesus. This is what the Apostle Peter was referring to when he preached on the day of Pentecost. He told the crowd that all who received Jesus Christ as their Lord and Savior would "receive the gift of the Holy Spirit. The promise is for you and your children and for all who are far off" (Acts 2:38-39).

Praise be to God who has given us a way to escape from the world's kingdom by being born again spiritually into the Kingdom of Heaven. This is what the Gospel of Jesus Christ is all about. "For he has rescued us from the dominion of darkness and brought us into the kingdom of the Son he loves, in whom we have redemption, the forgiveness of sins" (Colossians 1:13). "If you believe that Jesus is the Christ—that He is God's Son and your Savior—then you are a child of God. ... He has given us eternal life, and ... this life is in His Son. So whoever has God's Son has life; whoever does not have his Son, does not have life" (1 John 5:1, 11-12, The Living Bible). "For God so loved the world that he gave his one and only Son, that whoever believes in him shall not perish but have eternal life. For God did not send his Son into the world to condemn the world, but to save the world through him. Whoever believes in him is not condemned, but whoever does not believe stands condemned already because he has not believed in the name of God's one and only Son" (John 3:16-19).

WHY JESUS IS THE ONLY TRUTH THAT LEADS TO HEAVEN

We serve a loving and just God, whom the Bible says "wants all men to be saved and to come to a knowledge of the truth" (1 Timothy 2:4).

In today's world, there are many religions, even including groups falsely calling themselves Christians. We need to know the difference, because only one leads to Heaven. The **"knowledge of the truth"** the Bible speaks of in 1 Timothy 2:4 is given in the next verse. It states, **"For there is one God and one mediator between God and men, the man Christ Jesus."** True Christianity is based on the teach-

THE BIBLE SAYS GOD "WANTS ALL MEN TO BE SAVED."

ings of the Bible—and more specifically the Gospel of Jesus Christ. It is to experience a personal encounter—a personal relationship—with Him as Savior and Lord. This is the only truth that will take you to Heaven.

Though we may not understand all that happens in the spiritual world, it is when we accept God's Son, Jesus Christ, as our personal Lord and Savior that the power of God is released in our lives. We experience a spiritual rebirth, or new beginning, brought about by the Holy Spirit. We also become members of the Kingdom of God and Heaven. Scripture tells us that only those in the Kingdom of God will spend eternity with Him in that special heavenly place He has prepared.

There is in the world what I call "the religion of Christianity." Many people practice "the religion of Christianity," but it is not based upon the true Gospel of Jesus Christ. It directs our faith toward man-made concepts, just like the Pharisees and Sadducees did when Jesus was here on Earth. Our commitment for salvation cannot be to such things as religious doctrines, ordinances, traditions, structures, and personalities. It cannot be to anything other than Jesus Christ and His teachings as found in the Scriptures. This non-biblical pseudo-Christianity has brought about a great deal of confusion. More tragically, it has caused many people to miss being born again into the Kingdom of God, and therefore, to miss Heaven.

I would never point you in the direction of shallow Christianity that is not the true way. Heaven is far too valuable for that. Unfortunately, in today's religious environment it is easy for people to get involved in what may be <u>called</u> Christianity but does not actually involve a commitment to Jesus Christ and His teachings. There is a difference. Involvement only requires activity!

The Apostle Paul was involved full-time in the religion of his day, but he said, **"Whatever was to my profit I now consider loss for the sake of Christ. What is more, I consider everything a loss compared to the surpassing greatness of knowing Christ Jesus my Lord, for whose sake I have lost all things. I consider them rubbish, that I may gain Christ and be found in Him, not having a righteousness of my own that comes from the law** [being able to keep all of the commandments] **but that which is through faith in Christ"** (Philippians 3:7-9).

Jesus Christ is the true and living God who created all things, including you and me. When the Virgin Mary gave birth to Jesus, an angel said to the shepherds living out in the fields near His birthplace of Bethlehem, **"'Do not be afraid. I bring you good news of great joy that will be for all the people. Today in the town of David a Savior has been born to you; he is Christ the Lord. This will be a sign to you: You will find a baby wrapped in cloths and lying in a manger.' Suddenly a great company of the heavenly host appeared with the angel, praising God and saying, 'Glory to God in the highest, and on earth peace to men on whom his favor rests'"** (Luke 2:10-14). Jesus is the Savior for all who come to Him. He will save their souls from Hell. The angels knew how important this was for mankind; it was news of great joy!

The Word of God calls Jesus: **"The Alpha and the Omega"** (Revelation 1:8); **"Anointed"** (Psalms 2:2); **"Bread of Life"** (John 5:48); **"The Bright and Morning Star"** (Revelation 22:16); **"Chosen and Precious Cornerstone"** (I Peter 2:6); **"Wonderful Counselor"** (Isaiah 9:6); **"Mighty God"** (Isaiah 9:36); **"Deliverer"** (Romans 11:26); **"Emmanuel"** (Isaiah 7:14—which means God is with us); **"Eternal Life"** (I John 5:20); **"Firstborn"** (Psalms 89:27); **"Foundation"** (Isaiah 28:16);

"**Friend of Sinners**" (Matthew 11:19); "**Good Shepherd**" (John 10:11); "**High Priest**" (Hebrews 4:14); "**I Am**" (John 8:58); "**Our God**" (Isaiah 40:3); "**King of Kings**" (I Timothy 6:15); "**Lamb**" (Revelation 5:12); "**Light of the World**" (John 8:12); "**Living Bread**" (John 6:51); "**Messiah**" (John 1:41); "**Most Holy**" (Daniel 9:24); "**Physician**" (Matthew 9:12); "**Prince of Peace**" (Isaiah 9:6); "**Rabbi**" (John 1:49); "**Rock**" (I Corinthians 10:4); "**Rose of Sharon**" (Song of Songs 2:1); "**Descended from David**" (II Timothy 2:8); "**Sun of Righteousness**" (Malachi 4:2); "**Teacher**" (John 3:2); "**The Way, The Truth, The Life**" (John 14:6); "**Word**" (John 1:11). Jesus said, "**No one comes to the Father except through me**" (John 14:6).

In 1926 Dr. James Allen Francis wrote, "One Solitary Life." Let me share it.

> *Let us turn now to the story. A child is born in an obscure village. He is brought up in another obscure village. He works in a carpenter shop until he is thirty, and then for three brief years is an itinerant preacher, proclaiming a message and living a life. He never writes a book. He never holds an office. He never raises an army. He never has a family of his own. He never owns a home. He never goes to college. He never travels two hundred miles from the place where he was born. He gathers a little group of friends about him and teaches them his way of life. While still a young man, the tide of popular feeling turns against him. One denies him; another betrays him. He is turned over to his enemies. He goes through the mockery of a trail; he is nailed to a cross between two thieves, and when dead is laid in a borrowed grave by the kindness of a friend.*
>
> *Those are the facts of his human life. He rises from the dead. Today we look back across nineteen hundred years and ask, what kind of trail has he left across the centuries? When we try to sum up his influence, all the armies that ever marched, all the parliaments that ever sat, all the kings that ever reigned are absolutely picayune in their influence on mankind compared with that of this one solitary life.*

The earthly ministry of Jesus only lasted about three and a half years, yet the impact of His life on the history of mankind has been far greater than that of anyone else who ever lived. Why did Jesus have such an influence? He was God come to Earth in the form of a human being.

> OUR SALVATION IS NOT BASED ON OUR BEING GOOD ENOUGH, BUT ON THE RIGHTEOUSNESS OF JESUS CHRIST.

One of the problems people have in becoming a genuine Christian is they don't believe they can possibly be good enough. And they're right! No one ever is. We are all sinners, born into the kingdom of the world. We can't pile up good deeds and hope they will make us acceptable in God's sight. That is not the way to gain favor with God. Our salvation is <u>not</u> based on our being good enough, but on the righteousness of Jesus Christ. This is why **"salvation is found in no one else, for there is no other name under heaven given to men by which we must be saved"** (Acts 4:12).

Jesus is the only one who was ever good enough to qualify for Heaven. He lived a sinless life! It is through Him that people like you and me are made right with God—that is where we get the righteousness we need to be saved. That is why **"salvation is found in no one else"** as the verse states. <u>The righteousness of Jesus Christ is **credited to our account** in the eyes of God when we accept Jesus as our Lord and Savior.</u>

"But now a righteousness from God, apart from law (our keeping all of God's commandments and never sinning) **has been made known, to which the Law and the Prophets testify. <u>This righteousness from God comes through faith in Jesus Christ to all who believe</u>** [accept Him as Lord and Savior; emphasis added]. **There is no difference, for all have sinned and fall short of the glory of God, and are justified freely by his grace** [our salvation is a free gift]

through the redemption that came by Christ Jesus. God presented him as a sacrifice of atonement, through faith in his blood" (Romans 3:21-25).

God can't pretend sin doesn't exist. Yet because of His love for mankind, He sent His Son to break sin's condemning power over us and redeem us from the kingdom of the world. When Jesus shed His blood on the cross to pay the price for man's sins, He became the Savior of mankind and allowed us to escape from Satan's spiritual kingdom of the world. If we accept Jesus as Lord and Savior, God will apply the righteousness of Jesus Christ to our own record. That is how our relationship with God is changed. It is how we fit His standards and qualify for spiritual rebirth into the Kingdom of Heaven. It is not because of our goodness, but because of Jesus Christ's sinless life, death and resurrection. **"Know that a man is not justified by observing the law, but by faith in Jesus Christ ... because by observing the law** [never sinning but keeping all of God's commandments] **no one will be justified"** (Galatians 2:16).

Do we deserve this? No, it is because of God's grace. His great love for mankind made this marvelous provision of salvation from the world's kingdom and Hell available to us. It is a free gift from God. And best of all, it assures us of an eternity in Heaven. We should respond to such a gift by receiving it thankfully and with a repentant heart.

For all of those who know Jesus as their Savior, the grave has been transformed from a foe to a friend. With the backing of the Bible we can say, *"We need to have no fear of death."* Our last breath here will result in instantaneous, complete healing and exquisite joy on the other side in a better world. Jesus and Heaven are ours! In a word, sunset here is sunrise there! As Paul said, **"For to me, to live is Christ and to die is gain"** (Philippians 1:21).

To the natural person, death is the final pauperizing blow; to die is loss. Nothing bankrupts humans so completely as death. What a contrast is Paul's statement, **"To die is gain."** Only a Christian like Paul could say this with confidence based on certified guarantees. He knew, as we can know, how soundly factual the basis of the Christian faith really is.

What Heaven represents is unmistakable. To be there will be the highest fulfillment of all hopes. Gone forever will be the burdens of mortal flesh. There will be no more weakness, pain, temptation, grief, limitations or frustrations. Heaven is a place where there is no unholy thought, desire, fear, doubt or anxiety. No more hungering and thirsting; every tear wiped away; drinking "living waters" of immortality. Peter describes it as **"an inheritance that can never perish, spoil or fade"** (1 Peter 1:4).

> WE ALL HAVE
> TO CHOOSE BETWEEN
> HEAVEN AND HELL.

All around us will be those "clouds of witnesses"—the redeemed of all the centuries. The saints of the Old and New Testament will gather. Added to that will be a reunion with our departed loved ones. Every blemish, every disfigurement, every mark of age or weakness will be gone forever. There will be no fading of identity nor blurring of personality. You will always be you. I shall always be me.

No words can properly communicate all the riches God has in store for those who put their faith in His Son. We all have to choose between Heaven and Hell. Whichever one we decide on will be for eternity. Many people do not want to hear such a statement, or they ignore the reality that they ultimately have to make a choice. But if there is even a possibility of a Heaven and a Hell, it is far too critical a decision for anyone to pass off lightly, or to not try to find out all that it involves. That is poor judgment.

You do not want to miss Heaven.
God does not want you to miss Heaven.
I do not want you to miss Heaven.
You do not have to miss Heaven.

Is God's plan fair? It is more than fair! It required a great sacrifice on the part of both God the Father and the Son. Remember that it is mankind who turned his back on God; God never turned against mankind. We are the guilty party. God didn't have to save us! We should be thankful that He loved us enough to provide a plan so we might be saved from spending eternity in Hell, despite the fact that we often live contrary to His standards. The reason God's plan of salvation is a just one is that He took the burden upon Himself through His Son Jesus. Who can argue with that? What authority does mankind have to alter God's plan with one that is humanly-developed or created?

A portion of Scripture I find meaningful is in Romans 5:12-20. In essence what God's Word is saying is that because of one man, Adam's sin, all mankind inherited a sinful nature and therefore spiritual death or separation from God. The Bible also says therefore it is a right and just plan that mankind can be saved, reunited with God, by one man's righteousness, which was accomplished by Jesus Christ. **"Consequently, just as the result of one trespass was condemnation for all men, so also the result of one act of righteousness was justification that brings life for all men. For just as through the disobedience of the one man the many were made sinners, so also through the obedience of the one man the many will be made righteous"** (Romans 5:18-19).

A common question is what happens to children who die. Although all are born sin-infected and into the kingdom of the world, young children are not guilty. There is no such thing as inherited guilt. Those who die as children are not saved <u>by</u> their innocence but <u>because</u> of it. I believe the Bible teaches that we are not accountable for our transgressions until we reach a responsible age where we knowingly commit wrong. That, and only that, makes us transgressors and consequently guilty.

DECISION TIME

A poll taken of the American people by Marker Facts Telenation for *US News & World Report* appeared in the June 20, 1997 edition of

USA TODAY. It stated that eighty-eight percent of the adults in the U.S. who believe there is a Heaven also believe they will go to Heaven.

Why do so many believe they will go to Heaven? Are they basing their belief on what they hope is true rather than what they really know? In my opinion one reason people don't want to think they are <u>not</u> going to Heaven is because this is such an important issue. It is for eternity! Deep within they know there is a possibility it will either be Heaven or Hell.

Like it or not, each of us makes a decision that will determine our eternal state of being, even if it is by our silence. That may sound harsh, but it is the truth. All of us must pass over to that other side of the grave. To talk about death is not being morbid; it is rational, because death is inescapable. The Bible says there is coming a final Judgment Day and every person will stand before God. Those who are <u>not</u> believers in the Gospel of Jesus Christ are condemned. **"Whoever believes in him is not condemned, but whoever does not believe stands condemned already because he has not believed in the name of God's one and only Son"** (John 3:18).

That is actually a fearful thought! Every person should consider it seriously while the opportunity lingers. I am not playing on your emotions. I am addressing your intelligence, conscience, and free will. Death has a way of striking unexpectedly, and when it does, your final chance is gone. <u>There are no extra opportunities.</u> If you are an individual who has not done so, receive the risen Savior Jesus into your heart now. God loves every person, and His plan of salvation is available to everyone, regardless of what they may have done up to this point in their life. Few are worse than the Apostle Paul before he learned the truth of Jesus Christ. He hated the Gospel and was even a leader in killing Christians, but God transformed him.

Repent and accept Jesus Christ into your heart as Savior and Lord. That is what Paul did on the road to Damascus, and it is what millions of others have done. It is the only way to know for sure that you are going to Heaven. If you sincerely mean it, you will experience a spiritual rebirth into the Kingdom of Heaven. You will know that it happened, and you will be in the Kingdom of God and will inherit Heaven as well as many blessings in this life, which come from such a relationship that you now do not understand.

God knows you intimately, and He is not as concerned with your words as He is with the attitude of your heart. The following is a suggested prayer:

"Lord Jesus, I want to know You personally. Thank You for sacrificing Your life on the cross for my sins and making it possible for me to spend eternal life in Heaven. I open the door of my heart and receive You as my Savior and Lord. Take control of the throne of my life, and make me the kind of person You want me to be."

ACCEPTING JESUS CHRIST INTO YOUR HEART IS THE ONLY WAY TO KNOW FOR SURE THAT YOU ARE GOING TO HEAVEN.

If these words express the desire of your heart, pray this prayer right now. Christ will come into your life as He promised. It is then important that you locate a church that believes in and follows true biblical Christianity, so that you can be grounded in the Word of God and become active as salt and light in the world.

I have reviewed the basic plan of salvation and what we must do to be rescued from the kingdom of the world and be made a member of the Kingdom of God. **"And this is the testimony: God has given us eternal life, and this life is in his Son. He who has the Son has life; he who does not have the Son of God does not have life. I write these things to you who believe in the name of the Son of God so that you may know that you have eternal life"** (I John 5:11-13).

Next chapter I want to discuss some of the fundamental differences between the two spiritual kingdoms, the kingdom of the world and the Kingdom of Heaven. This knowledge will help us understand the prophetic Scriptures that warn about the attack methods Satan is using in these last days of the Church Age.

QUESTIONS FOR GROUP DISCUSSION AND/OR TO BE ANSWERED INDIVIDUALLY

Explain in your own words what it means to be "born again" spiritually.

_____

_____

_____

_____

_____

_____

In what ways might it be possible to be in a Christian church and still not be a true Christian?

_____

_____

_____

_____

_____

_____

I state that we should ask Jesus to be both our Savior and Lord. What is the difference between these two concepts?

_____

_____

_____

_____

Where are you in this matter of choosing to leave the "kingdom of the world" to become a part of the "Kingdom of God"?

_____

_____

_____

_____

_____

How do these two opposite kingdoms relate to a person's eternal destiny?

_____

_____

_____

_____

_____

How do Jesus' teachings about salt and light relate to these two different kingdoms?

_____

_____

_____

_____

_____

CHAPTER FOUR

THE TWO SPIRITUAL KINGDOMS

SPIRITUAL KINGDOM
OF THE WORLD

I was somewhat amazed to find that the word *world* is used more than 200 times in the New Testament. That's more frequently than *love* or *Holy Spirit* appear. God must have felt it quite important that we clearly understand its meaning. The Greek word in Scripture for *world* is *kosmos*. It has three primary uses:

One: To reference the material universe or Earth. **"I will open my mouth in parables, I will utter things hidden since the creation of the <u>world</u>"** (Matthew 13:35).

Two: To reference the inhabitants or people of the world. **"For God so loved the <u>world</u> that He gave His one and only Son, that whoever believes in Him shall not perish, but have eternal life"** (John 3:16).

Three: To reference the moral and spiritual systems we call <u>society</u>. It's that realm of the world developed through human effort rather than created by God. It consists of political and governmental systems, economic and financial systems, educational systems, religious systems, entertainment systems, legal systems, medicine, the arts, science and technology, and so forth. Eliminate such elements, and you do away with a society. The Bible refers to this third use when it says that Satan is the world's ruler. **"We know that we** [Christians] **are children of God, and that the whole world** [societies] **is under the control of the evil one"** (1 John 5:19).

Until a person has been born again, he or she is a member of the kingdom of the world, which is under Satan's spiritual influence. Most of what has been developed by mankind falls into the realm of the kingdom of the world. They are not of God's Kingdom; i.e., they are not under the control and influence of the Holy Spirit. **"As for you, you were dead in your transgressions and sins, in which you used to live when you followed the ways of this world, and the ruler of the kingdom of the air, the spirit** [Satan] **who is now at work in those who are disobedient. All of us also lived among them at one time, gratifying the cravings of our sinful nature, and following its desires and thoughts. Like the rest, we were by nature** [born this way] **objects of wrath. But because of his great love for us, God, who is rich in mercy, made us alive with Christ even when we were dead in transgressions—it is by grace you have been saved"** (Ephesians 2:1-5).

> ELEMENTS OF
> THE WORLD CAN BE
> CONVERTED FOR
> THE GLORY OF GOD.

So there is a mind behind society—a controlling spiritual influence—referred to in the Bible as the "prince of this world" and "he that is in the world." **"For we are not fighting against people made of flesh and blood, but against persons without bodies—the evil rulers of the unseen world, those mighty satanic beings and great evil princes of darkness who rule this world; and against huge numbers of wicked spirits in the spirit world"** (Ephesians 6:12, The Living Bible). When Satan tempted Jesus, he **"took Him up and revealed to Him all the**

kingdoms of the <u>world</u> in a moment of time. And the Devil told Him, 'I will give you all these splendid kingdoms and their glory—for they are mine to give to anyone I wish'" (Luke 4:5-6, TLB). Jesus did not contest Satan's claim of authority over the kingdoms of this world.

This is not to say that elements of the world cannot be converted and used for the glory of God, just as man can be. But on the whole, God warns us that our spiritual enemy controls these systems that make up society. This is important to remember, because the world system is one of Satan's key attack vehicles to tempt Christians and wage spiritual warfare against them. It is through these that he often keeps Christians from fulfilling God's mission to be the **salt of the earth** and the **light of the world**.

This is why we find several Scriptures of warning: **"Do not conform any longer to the pattern of this <u>world</u>** (society)**, but be transformed by the renewing of your mind. Then you will be able to test and approve what God's will is"** (Romans 12:2). **Religion that God, our Father, accepts as pure and faultless is this: to look after orphans and widows in their distress <u>and to keep oneself from being polluted</u>** (spotted) **<u>by the world</u>** (society)**"** (James 1:27). **"You adulterous people, don't you know that friendship with the <u>world</u>** (society) **is hatred toward God? Anyone who chooses to be a friend of the <u>world</u>** (society) **becomes an enemy of God"** (James 4:4). **"Do not love the <u>world</u>** [become attached to the things of society] **or anything in the <u>world</u>. If anyone loves the <u>world</u>, the love of the Father is not in him. For everything in the <u>world</u> comes not from the Father** [they are under Satan's influence] **but from the world"** (1 John 2:15-16). **"Finally, be strong in the Lord and in his mighty power. Put on the full armor of God so that you can take your stand against the devil's schemes. For our struggle is not against flesh and blood, but against rulers, against the authorities, against the powers of this dark <u>world</u>** (societies)**"** (Ephesians 6:10-12).

Jesus and the Apostle Paul sum up the Christian's position in the world. Jesus said, **"If the <u>world</u> hates you, keep in mind that it hated** me first. **If you belonged to the <u>world</u>, it would love you as its own. As it is, you do not belong to the <u>world</u>, but <u>I have chosen you out of the world</u>** (the spiritual kingdom of the world). **That is why the <u>world</u> hates you**" (John 15:18-19). Paul calls himself spiritually dead to the world: "**May I never boast except in the cross of our Lord Jesus Christ, through which the <u>world</u> has been crucified to me, and I to the <u>world</u>**" (Galatians 6:14).

THERE ARE STRONG WARNINGS IN SCRIPTURE ABOUT SOCIETY.

After we have been born again, we too are dead to the kingdom of the world and alive in God's Kingdom. Our function here on Earth is to represent His Kingdom, to be a shining **light** and a preservative **salt**. There is a reason why there are such strong warnings in Scripture about society or the kingdom of the world. Although we have been **"rescued ... from the dominion of darkness and brought ... into the kingdom of the Son he loves"** (Colossians 1:13), Christians still retain the sinful nature we are born with. God knows that after we become Christians, Satan will constantly tempt our sinful nature, using the kingdom of the world as his vehicle. In this sense we are in spiritual warfare every day!

Society is one of **Satan's main attack vehicles**. We need only look at our own society in recent years to know this to be true. One of the reasons for the change in America has come through the influence of electronic media such as TV, movies and the Internet. They barge right into our homes every minute of the day. This fallout has affected our schools, our businesses, even our churches.

Sinful Nature

After becoming a Christian, Paul discovered the truth that mankind has a sinful nature, which he called the law of sin (see Romans 7:18-8:2). The characteristics of the kingdom of the world include: **lovers**

of ourselves and of money but not of good, pride, boastful, abu-sive, disobedience, rebellion, permissiveness, ungratefulness, immorality, unforgiveness, slander, lack of self-control, cruelty, treachery, rashness, conceit, anger, jealousy, and lovers of pleasure rather than God (see 2 Timothy 3:2-4). This is not to say that all of these qualities are a part of every human being all the time. Some of these will only be displayed in our personalities under certain circumstances, while others are determined by the society in which we are raised and what is considered acceptable by its standards.

These natural tendencies that make up the sinful nature we are born with cause us to emphasize personality, natural abilities, appearance, family heritage, nationality, intelligence, wealth, worldly position and authority. It is our sinful nature that promotes self-reliance, self-confidence, self-expression, self-exaltation, self-glorification and self-satisfaction rather than our complete dependence on God, which is what Jesus lived and taught. Paul knew that in his sinful nature he was a wretched man, but because he had accepted Jesus as his Savior, he was no longer condemned but had been set free. He declared, **"What a wretched man I am! Who will rescue me from this body of death? Thanks be to God—through Jesus Christ our Lord! So then, I myself in my mind am a slave to God's law, but in the sinful nature a slave to the law of sin. Therefore, there is now no condemnation for those who are in Christ Jesus, because through Christ Jesus the law of the Spirit of life set me free from the law of sin and death"** (Romans 7:24-8:2).

> UNDERSTANDING
> OUR SINFUL NATURE
> IS CRUCIAL.

Understanding our sinful nature is critical to understanding the prophetic Scriptures about the last days and how Satan is attacking Christians. Our old sinful nature is too easily carried over into the Kingdom of God. Although we are new creatures in Christ, this law of our sinful nature remains with us. We do not lose it! Through our own personal experiences, all of us can identify with Paul's realization.

UNDERSTANDING THE ELEMENTS OF OUR SINFUL NATURE

There are <u>three main elements that make up our self-serving sinful nature</u> that are especially subject to Satan's temptations. John lists them: **"Do not love the world** [society] **or the things in the world. If anyone loves the world, love for the Father is not in him. For all that is in the world, <u>the lust of the flesh</u> and <u>the lust of the eyes</u> and <u>the pride of life</u>, is not of the Father but is of the world"** (1 John 2:15-16, RSV).

It was these three elements that Satan used to deceive Eve and then Adam. **"When the woman saw that the fruit of the tree was good for food** [lust of the flesh] **and pleasing to the eye** [lust of the eyes]**, and also desirable for gaining wisdom** [pride of life]**, she took some and ate it. She also gave some to her husband, who was with her, and he ate it"** (Genesis 3:6). God had told Adam and Eve not to eat the fruit of this particular tree or they would die. After they disobeyed, **"the Lord God said to the woman, 'What is this you have done?' The woman said, 'The serpent** [Satan] **deceived me, and I ate'"** (Genesis 3:13).

As you explore the Bible and examine the reasons why men of God like Samson, Saul, David, Solomon and others fell into sin, you will discover that they fell in one or more of these three areas: the lust of the flesh, the lust of the eyes and the pride of life. It was with these same three self-serving attractions that Satan tried to trap and deceive Jesus (see Luke 4:1-12). If you examine why spiritual leaders and lay-people are falling into sin today, the basic cause is still these same three elements that John warns us about.

It is critical to keep these three in mind when we examine how Satan is carrying out his spiritual warfare in these last days, especially against America. We learn from prophetic Scriptures that Satan will attempt to destroy every spiritual influence in our nation, to keep Christians from fulfilling our end-times mission to be **salt** and **light**.

There is a part of our natural makeup that is attracted by what is sinful. Satan is fully aware of the nature that man is born with, <u>the lust of the flesh, the lust of the eyes and the pride of life</u>. Notice how often these three are at the core of entertainment and advertising as we go about our lives.

KINGDOM OF GOD AND HEAVEN

As I now write about the Kingdom of God, note what a vast contrast it is to the kingdom of the world. When we are born again by the Spirit, we are redeemed from the kingdom of the world and become members of the Kingdom of God. We are a new spiritual creation. **"Therefore, if anyone is in Christ, he is a new creation the old has gone** (being a member of the kingdom of the world), **the new has come** (being a member of the Kingdom of God)!"** (II Corinthians 5:17). We have entered into a kingdom with completely different characteristics, principles, and standards from those that make up the kingdom of the world. Most of the New Testament is written to help us learn how to thrive in this new Kingdom. The Scriptures are like a road map to guide us, and the Holy Spirit lives in us to transform our old nature into God's new nature. This change is an ongoing process that will continue for the rest of our lives. As we grow in the Lord, there will always be areas where we are not as spiritually mature as we could be.

It is a glorious adventure to serve the Lord. I was raised in a strong Christian family as the youngest of 13 children. At age nine I accepted Jesus as my personal Savior. I had a close walk with the Lord during most of my teens, but fell away from my strong commitment in my twenties. When we were nearly 30, my wife and I recommitted our lives to serve the Lord.

The Apostle Paul stated, **"Therefore, I urge you, brothers, in view of God's mercy, to offer your bodies as living sacrifices, holy and pleasing to God—which is your spiritual worship"** (Romans 12:1). As a new member of the Kingdom of God we are a temple of the Holy Spirit. We are not our own anymore; we were bought at a price by Christ's blood. This world is no longer our primary home. This doesn't mean that we should not work, play and raise our families in this world, but as Jesus said, **"You do not belong to the world, but I have chosen you out of the world"** (John 15:19).

Jesus gave us the ruling characteristics of His Kingdom and then demonstrated how they are to be carried out by those who belong to Him. These are found in the greatest sermon ever preached, The Sermon on the Mount (see Matthew 5-7). It is the one place that gives us an overview of the characteristics of this heavenly Kingdom. It was also in this sermon that Jesus said we are to be the **salt of the earth** and the **light of the world**.

SERMON ON THE MOUNT

Nowhere else in the Bible is the new lifestyle of a Christian more clearly outlined than the Sermon on the Mount. The teachings in this sermon lay out the qualities of the characteristics that governed the life of Jesus. In other words, it tells us what it means to be Christ-like. As the Apostle Paul said, Jesus **"gave himself for us to redeem us from all wickedness and to purify for himself a people that are his very own, eager to do what is good"** (Titus 2:14).

As we focus on the first part of this Sermon, called the Beatitudes, you will quickly see that it would crush us if we had to live this way through our own strength. How utterly helpless we are without the gracious operation of the Holy Spirit.

The word **"blessed"** before each of these characteristics that Jesus gives us of the Kingdom of God means <u>happy</u>. **"Blessed** [happy] **are the**

poor in spirit, for theirs is the kingdom of heaven. Blessed [happy]
are those who mourn, for they will be comforted. Blessed [happy]
are the meek, for they will inherit the earth. Blessed [happy] **are**
those who hunger and thirst for righteousness, for they will be
filled. Blessed [happy] **are the merciful, for they will be shown**
mercy. Blessed [happy] **are the pure in heart, for they will see God.**
Blessed [happy] **are the peacemakers, for they will be called sons of**
God" (Matthew 5:3-9).

The poor in spirit, those who mourn, the meek, anyone hungry and
thirsty for righteousness, the merciful, the pure in heart and peacemakers—these are the ones who are blessed. In the next chapter I will
explain the meaning of each of these. For now, note that Jesus lists these
qualities just a few verses before He makes His declaration that we are
to be the **salt of the earth** and
the **light of the world**. I believe
He is telling us that developing
these spiritual characteristics is a
prerequisite for fulfilling the call
to be salt and light.

It is also important to know
that Satan's warfare against
Christians is designed to prevent
the development of these special
characteristics in our lives. He is
going to do every thing he can,

> SATAN'S WARFARE
> IS DESIGNED TO
> PREVENT THE
> DEVELOPMENT OF
> THESE SPECIAL
> CHARACTERISTICS.

using the things of the world or society, to keep these characteristics at
a minimum in their development in Christians. Our knowing this is
another key to help us understand the spiritual warfare now taking
place in America.

Another obvious reason why it is good to review these Beatitudes is
that the more we live them, along with the rest of the Sermon's teachings,
the more we will experience God's blessings and be happy. We don't have
to seek some other method. Other options don't work anyway!

Finally, we should study this sermon because as we live it out, our lives will become a powerful witness. If all Christians lived as Jesus taught in this Sermon, we would see men and women crowding into our church buildings.

The Sermon on the Mount has two subdivisions. First is the general part, in Matt. 5:3-16. Here Jesus makes statements regarding the Christian character. In the rest of the sermon He gives examples of how these are lived out.

AN OVERVIEW OF THE SPIRITUAL CHARACTERISTICS THAT RULE GOD'S KINGDOM

The following are a few general comments about each of these Beatitudes.

One: These characteristics apply to all Christians. We have a tendency to divide believers into two separate groups when it comes to character: the church leaders, or pastors, and the laity, or the ordinary folk who are involved in secular affairs. That thinking is unscriptural.

There is distinction in offices—apostles, prophets, teachers, pastors and so on. But the Beatitudes are a description of spiritual character. They do not apply just to the Hudson Taylors, George Müllers, John Wesleys, Charles Finneys, D. L. Moodys or Billy Grahams. These are the spiritual characteristics that are to mark every Christian.

Two: Every one of these characteristics is to be manifested in every Christian. For example, some Christians are <u>not</u> meant to manifest 3 or 4 of these spiritual characteristics, while others demonstrate a different 3 or 4. These Beatitudes describe a completeness of character, and you really can't divide them up.

Three: Very important. These characteristics do not refer to what we might call natural ability. Each depends upon grace alone and the work of the Holy Spirit. No one can conform to the description of any of these spiritual characteristics, let alone all of them, by the natural power of the flesh.

There are people who may appear to possess one or more of these characteristics who may not be a Christian. But just as people differ in their physical appearance, they differ in their natural temperament. That is not what Jesus is describing. These characteristics are spiritual, developed by the Holy Spirit and have nothing to do with our natural biological temperament.

Four: These spiritual characteristics indicate the essential difference between the non-Christian and the Christian—the difference between those in the kingdom of the world and those in the Kingdom of God. Today this distinction has become blurred; the world has come into the Church, and as a result the Church has become worldly. There are those today who believe you have to make the church more worldly in order to attract people from the outside. When we do this, we just end up with worldly Christians!

A simple graph illustrates how the standards Christians live by in our society have systematically been lowered in recent years.

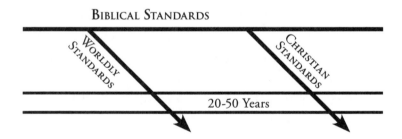

As illustrated by the top line, biblical standards always remain the same. The line on the left shows how worldly standards in our society have been deteriorating. The line on the right reveals that over the same period of time Christian standards have also been lowered. This has come about because many have set our Christian standards by comparing them to the world's, rather than by using only biblical truths. We have maintained the same distance between the world's standards, we are not as bad as the world, but this false comparison is a trick of the enemy. It has caused us to lower Christian standards. The net result is that what was considered a worldly standard in American society 20 to 30 years ago has now become acceptable for many Christians.

This deceptive work of Satan has caused us to become more tolerant regarding many of the sins described in the Bible. It has devastated the lives of many Christians, because sin always leads to broken lives. The Bible puts it very bluntly: **"The wages of sin is death"** (Romans 6:23). This truth does not only apply to salvation. Sin is a frequent cause for the inner hurt and pain so many in the church suffer.

A WORLDLY STANDARD IN AMERICAN SOCIETY 20 TO 30 YEARS AGO HAS NOW BECOME ACCEPTABLE FOR MANY CHRISTIANS.

For the moral character of the people in the world to change is understandable. History reveals the majority of non-Christians usually follow the trends of a society, but for Christians it's supposed to be different. We are new creations, born again into the Kingdom of God to be the righteousness of God. As with Eve, then Adam, Satan's scheme of **spiritual deception** has been highly successful in America in this past generation. This is evident as the world's moral standards has had a greater influence on us in this generation than Christian standards has had on the world. Not only is this illustrated by the above graph, but also by the moral fruit produced in our society and in the body of Christ. Keep in mind that **deception** is determined by the fruit being produced.

I would rather dwell on the positives than the negatives. But when we see that we are continually losing the battle, we cannot continue to hide our heads in the sand. We need to take corrective action and confront the negative issues. To dwell on the positives and ignore the truth of the negatives may sound good, but doing so only touches lives temporarily rather than permanently.

The glory of the gospel is that when the church is absolutely different from the world, it invariably attracts outsiders. The world may hate the message at first, but it has been proven time and again that people will listen when they see a true difference. That is how revival comes. This same principle applies to each individual Christian. Our ambition should not be to fit in with everybody else, but to be different, even as Jesus was. We belong to a different Kingdom, and our aim is to be like the Ruler of that Kingdom. The more we are like Him, the better. And the more like Him we become, the more we will be <u>unlike</u> those who are still members of the kingdom of the world.

We are not here to make sure we get everything we can out of this present experience. The Christian life is different. We are not to live for the world, but regard it, or society, as that which we are passing through into something vast and eternal and glorious. Peter states, **"Dear friends, I urge you, as aliens and strangers in the world, to abstain from sinful desires, which war against your soul. Live such good lives among the pagans that though they accuse you of doing wrong, they may see your good deeds and glorify God on the day he visits us"** (1 Peter 2:11-12). The sinful desires that Peter mentions include all kinds of earthly wishes: **the lust of the eyes, the lust of the flesh and the pride of life**.

The Bible teaches that Satan's objective is to use every conceivable sensual desire to tempt us away from living a victorious Christian life. We see how he uses the things of the world to the ruin of those of the world. But we are seeking a heavenly home, and should not set our affections on earthly things. We are not like those who live in the kingdom of darkness while neglecting the salvation of their souls.

Points to Remember from the Beatitudes About the Spiritual Characteristics of a Christian

1. Each of these spiritual characteristics applies to all Christians.
2. All Christians are meant to manifest every one of these characteristics.
3. None of these descriptions of Christian character refers to what we would call a natural tendency. They all are spiritual qualities and are only developed through the power of the Holy Spirit.

4. These descriptive Christian characteristics indicate the difference between the character of a Christian and the non-Christian.
5. These characteristics teach us the truth that the Christian and non-Christian belong to two entirely different kingdoms.

The first and the last promise given in these characteristics offer the same reward—**"for theirs is the kingdom of heaven."** We are here on Earth; we obey the laws of the land, as the Scriptures tell us we are to do. We work, play and raise our families in the ways the Lord directs. We live our lives here, but our true citizenship is in Heaven. Paul states, **"For he has rescued us from the dominion of darkness and brought us into the kingdom of the Son he loves"** (Colossians 1:13). And **"But our citizenship is in heaven. And we eagerly await a Savior from there, the Lord Jesus Christ, who, by the power that enables him to bring everything under his control, will transform our lowly bodies so that they will be like his glorious body"** (Philippians 3:20).

We should not get into a materialistic way of thinking about the Kingdom of God as the Jews did. They were looking for an earthly king and expected the Messiah would return them to political and military power as in the glory days of King David. Our Lord's objective in His teachings was to show that His Kingdom is primarily a spiritual one. To the disciples He sent out to preach, Jesus said to tell the cities that did not receive them, **"Be sure of this, that the kingdom of God is come nigh unto you"** (Luke 10:11, KJV). Wherever the reign of Christ is manifested, His Kingdom is there. The Kingdom of God is present at this very moment in all of us who are true believers. We represent the Kingdom of God in this world, and are not to live like citizens of the kingdom of the world.

Lastly, we need to remember that these characteristics are a mirror for us to look at ourselves—not something that we use to judge others. I will be the first to admit that I have not arrived in the development of these characteristics. Also, these are not a new moral code by which we become a member of the Kingdom of God. **"It is by grace you**

have been saved, through faith—and this not from yourselves, it is the gift of God—not by works, so that no one can boast" (Ephesians 2:8). Jesus gave these to us so we would know what the spiritual characteristics are that make up His Kingdom.

Now we are ready to examine how we are meant to live as citizens of God's Kingdom. As we do, I think you will understand why I believe we are in one of the toughest times ever to live the committed Christian life and carry out our mission of being the **salt of the earth** and the **light of the world**.

QUESTIONS FOR GROUP DISCUSSION AND/OR
TO BE ANSWERED INDIVIDUALLY

Why were many Jewish people in New Testament times confused regarding the Kingdom of God that Jesus preached about?

_____

_____

_____

_____

_____

_____

What are the clear distinctions between the kingdom of the world and the Kingdom of God? Name several reasons why today's Christians need to be aware of and understand this.

_____

_____

_____

_____

_____

_____

What does the statement I wrote, "There is a mind behind society—a controlling spiritual influence," mean to you?

_____

_____

_____

_____

What three elements make up our sinful nature? Give examples of each one.

_____

_____

_____

_____

_____

Give examples of the way Satan uses elements of society as his vehicle to attack our sinful nature.

_____

_____

_____

_____

Even after a person has been born again, why is one's sinful nature still a problem?

_____

_____

_____

_____

List specific ways biblical standards in America have been compromised by today's worldly standards.

_____

_____

_____

_____

What are the five points to remember about the spiritual characteristics of a Christian?

_____

_____

_____

_____

_____

_____

_____

_____

_____

_____

_____

CHAPTER FIVE

SPIRITUAL CHARACTERISTICS
OF THE KINGDOM OF GOD

Jesus told us how to be truly blessed or happy. The world longs for happiness, but many people seek it through sinful pursuits. It is tragic the many ways people seek happiness by getting involved in activities that only bring it for a short time. In the long run, what they usually find is misery.

Developing the spiritual traits Jesus taught is like climbing a rugged mountain. As we ascend our spiritual mountain God is working in us by burning out our old nature and developing these first three characteristics that Jesus lists—being **poor in spirit**, **mourning** and **meekness**—which makes us conscious of a <u>deep need</u> we have.

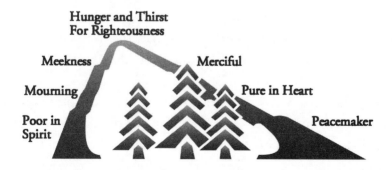

The development of these initial three characteristics causes us to **hunger and thirst after righteousness**. God promises to satisfy this hunger and thirst in that we **"shall be filled."** The result of this filling develops the last three spiritual characteristics as we descend our spiritual mountain. We will become **merciful, pure in heart, and peacemakers**. After that, Jesus warns, we may be **"persecuted because of righteousness"** as Satan hates and wars against the development of these godly characteristics. In later chapters as we discuss the prophetic Scriptures of Satan overcoming Christians in these last days, keep in mind how the influence of our society has made it extremely difficult for these basic Christian characteristics to be developed.

DEVELOPMENT OF CHRISTIAN CHARACTER

God develops our Christian character in three steps: need, satisfaction and results. First, He makes us aware of our need; next, He fills that need as we hunger and thirst for righteousness; and finally, He satisfies our longing by developing in us the qualities of mercy, being pure in heart, and a peacemaker. He is the potter; we are the clay. We are dependent on Jesus to deliver us from who we are and to develop in us the characteristics of His Kingdom.

We not only need Jesus for the salvation of our soul; we also need Him to deliver us from what we are. Jesus is everything, and everything is in Jesus.

SPIRITUAL CHARACTERISTIC NUMBER ONE
"Blessed are the poor in spirit, for theirs is the kingdom of heaven" (Matthew 5:3)

This heart characteristic is the keystone of all the other qualities. It deals with the process of emptying us of our old sinful nature so we can be filled with the power of God's new nature. The extent to which we become poor in spirit affects how successfully we develop the subsequent traits, and each characteristic builds on the previous ones.

The characteristic of being poor in spirit deals with a person's attitude toward self. The kingdom of this world promotes self-reliance, self-confidence, self-expression, self-exaltation and self-satisfaction. The world emphasizes personality, talent, looks, heritage, intelligence, wealth, power, etc. But the gospel raises up a higher standard that focuses on God-reliance, God-confidence, God-expression, God-exaltation and the desire to please God through obedience to His Word, His will and His way. It is a characteristic that is despised by the world.

Being poor in spirit does not mean suppressing one's true personality, trying to appear humble, making great sacrifices, or fleeing from the difficulties of everyday life. That certainly was not the way of Jesus.

The Scriptures define poor in spirit: **"The sacrifices of God are a broken spirit; a broken and contrite heart, O God, you will not despise"** (Psalm 51:17). **"For this is what the high and lofty One says—he who lives forever, whose name is holy: I live in a high and holy place, but also with him who is contrite and lowly in spirit, to revive the spirit of the lowly and to revive the heart of the contrite"** (Isaiah 57:15).

The characteristic **poor in spirit** means:

- We shall not rely on the fact that we belong to a given family.
- We shall not boast that we are a certain nationality.
- We shall not brag about our position in life, or any powers that may have been given to us.
- We shall not put confidence in the wealth we may have.
- We shall not flaunt our education.
- We shall not rely primarily on our personality, intelligence or special abilities.
- We shall not point to our morality and good behavior.
- We shall not build upon natural temperament.

To be poor in spirit is to be delivered from all that which promotes self. It is to know that within the flesh we are nothing, we have nothing, and we must look to God in utter dependence upon His grace and mercy. Within the flesh we are empty and hopeless, but He is the all-sufficient one.

How does one become **poor in spirit**? We do <u>not</u> begin by trying to do things to ourselves like sacrificing the flesh or suffering hardships. These only make us more conscious of ourselves and thus <u>less</u> **poor in spirit**. No, we must look to God. Our responsibility is to study God's Word to learn what He expects from us, and then to set our face as a flint to live in obedience. As we look at Him we feel our absolute poverty and, like the apostles, we cry out, "Lord, increase our faith."

The development of all these inner characteristics will evolve in us by the power of the Holy Spirit as we grow spiritually. They are characteristics of the Kingdom of God. You will see none of them are a part of our natural make-up.

Spiritual Characteristic Number Two
"Blessed are those who mourn, for they will be comforted" (Matthew 5:4)

This characteristic develops in us the honesty to see sin in ourselves and in the world as it really is. Christians are to be unlike the people of the world who try to shun **mourning**. Think of all the energy and money spent by the world system to blind people from this spiritual quality. As mourning becomes a part of our being, it causes us to see not only what sin does to people, but how it must stab God in the heart. I have heard it said that just the sin of using God's name in vain takes place more than one billion times every day in our country.

There has been a defection in the church from teaching on the doctrine of sin. This shows how much the world has influenced us. In most any other aspect of life, we concentrate on those areas where we are weakest. If we have a health problem, we try to resolve it. If we play sports, we focus on those areas where our performance is poor. The same is true in business.

Spiritually, mankind's weakness is sin! Why do we get so uptight talking about it? It doesn't have to be in a negative condemning way, but for positive solutions. We have a spiritual problem because we are born with a sinful nature. That is who we are! We need to face this truth and talk about it! Otherwise we will not let God deal with those areas where we are weak.

Paul mourned over the sinful condition of his flesh and looked forward to that day when it would be redeemed. **"But we ourselves, who have the first fruits of the Spirit, groan inwardly as we wait eagerly for our adoption as sons, the redemption of our bodies"** (Romans 8:23).

Mourning applies not only to our own sins, but also to the sins of others and the state of society and the world. When this characteristic is developed, we will mourn over the immorality, the suffering and the evil deeds of mankind. True happiness and joy can only come after mourning. That is one of the paradoxes of the Christian life.

Spiritual Characteristic Number Three
"Blessed are the meek, for they will inherit the earth"
(Matthew 5:5)

Meekness is often regarded as similar to being **poor in spirit**; however, it is quite different. Meekness is more difficult and more humbling than the previous two. It is also more searching, because it takes us from within ourselves to our relationship with others. I can evaluate, even condemn, myself, but when others do it, I tend to be resentful. Meekness is measured by how we respond when others put the spotlight on us.

Jesus took on the form of a servant and submitted to the will of His Father. He did not try to use the political systems of His day to accomplish God's mission. Instead He sacrificed Himself, giving His all in meekness to His Father's will. That is how meekness works.

One of the greatest leaders of all time was Moses. In Numbers 12:3 he is described as a meek man. He had been groomed and trained to be a leader in Egypt. Yet God chose to strip Moses of his self-power, position and abilities. His mission could only be accomplished through the character and power of God.

In his relationship with King Saul, David did not assert himself, though he could have on several occasions. As this Christian characteristic of meekness develops it causes us <u>not</u> to demand anything for ourselves in our relationships with others. When people scorn us or lie about us, we don't have to fight back and defend ourselves. It is not important that we assert our rights, position in life or privileges in relationship to others. No longer do we have to go on the defensive for the purpose of needing to be right. Our self-life has been crucified. It is no longer I who lives, but Christ who lives in me (see Galatians 2:20).

This does not mean that we are to be flabby, lacking in firmness, vigor, weak in personality, always exhibiting a compromising spirit. That is not how Jesus or Paul lived. They knew their mission and set their face as a flint to accomplish it; not in their own strength but through the power of God.

SPIRITUAL CHARACTERISTIC NUMBER FOUR
"Blessed are those who hunger and thirst for righteousness, for they will be filled"
(Matthew 5:6)

As we grow spiritually in the Lord, He must do away with our old nature as He develops in us a new one with these Christ-like characteristics. As the first three are formed in us, we are gradually emptied of **our old sinful nature**. Only then will we desire to be filled with God's righteousness, and the Lord will develop that desire into a hunger and thirst.

Righteousness is simply right living before God. **"The law of the Lord is perfect, reviving the soul. The statutes of the Lord are trustworthy, making wise the simple. The precepts of the Lord are right, giving joy to the heart. The commands of the Lord are radiant, giving light to the eyes. The fear of the Lord is pure, enduring forever. The ordinances of the Lord are sure and altogether righteous. They are more precious than gold. ... In keeping them there is much reward"** (Psalm 19:7-11).

Note that Jesus did <u>not</u> say to hunger and thirst after happiness or blessings. These come as a *result* of seeking righteousness. To hunger and thirst is to have the consciousness of a deep and desperate need, to the point that we experience pain in our soul. This brings suffering and agony, because it is an all-out drive to achieve the desired goal. It is somewhat like being away from home and homesick, or the inner drive people have to be a sports champion.

Hungering and thirsting for righteousness is the defining spiritual trait of our Christianity. If we truly desire righteousness, God's Spirit will transform us into His image. We cannot obtain it by our own efforts. Attempting to do so will only lead to pride, which has been the downfall of many throughout the history of Christianity.

Jesus promised that if we hunger and thirst for righteousness, we <u>will</u> be filled. This comes through the anointing power of the Holy Spirit. If one is emptied of a self-seeking nature and filled with God's nature, the next three characteristics given by Jesus—**merciful, pure in heart** and **peacemaker**—will flow naturally as we come down the mountain to minister for His Kingdom rather than for selfish reasons.

SPIRITUAL CHARACTERISTIC NUMBER FIVE
"Blessed are the merciful, for they will be shown mercy" (Matthew 5:7)

As these characteristics on the other side of the mountain become a natural part of our being, we start to express the true character of God. **Mercy** is a sense of pity <u>plus</u> an effort to relieve suffering. It is not pity alone; it includes <u>action</u>. Consider the Parable of the Good Samaritan. Others may have pitied the injured man, but they did nothing. They were not demonstrating mercy. Mercy allowed Jesus to see the miserable consequences of sin. It is also what drove Him to relieve the suffering sin causes both in this life and the life after death.

The characteristic of mercy develops a sacrificial love that inspires a person to do all he or she can to save another from the fiery pits of Hell.

We can be thankful we have a merciful God. He knows the consequences of sin. **"For God so loved the world** (mankind) **that he gave his one and only Son, that whoever believes in him** [accepts Him as Savior] **shall not perish** [spend eternity in Hell] **but have eternal life** [spend eternity in Heaven]. **For God did not send his Son into the world to condemn the world, but to save the world through him"** (John 3:16-17).

Mercy differentiates between the sinner and sin. God hates sin, but loves the sinner. Mercy causes us to see people as creatures to be pitied—slaves to a sinful nature—who are trapped in Satan's world system and suffering the awful consequences of sin. Even while He was on the cross, mercy moved Jesus to pray for His oppressors, **"Father, forgive them, for they do not know what they are doing"** (Luke 23:34).

Spiritual Characteristic Number Six
"Blessed are the pure in heart, for they will see God"
(Matthew 5:8)

Pure in Heart

Christian doctrine emphasizes the heart! Jesus baffled the scholars of His day because He bypassed the intellectual mechanics of the Scriptures and zeroed in on their effect on the heart. The Pharisees were interested in the outside more than the inside. They made the way of life and righteousness a mere matter of conduct and ethics.

"Heart" refers to the core of our being. It includes our mind, will and emotions. It is also the seat of all our problems. Jesus put it this way: **"For from within, out of men's hearts, come evil thought, sexual immorality, theft, murder, and adultery, greed, malice, deceit, lewdness, envy, slander, arrogance and folly. All these evils come from inside and make a man 'unclean'"** (Mark 7:20-23).

Even if we had a perfect environment, it would not solve man's problems. It was in paradise, the Garden of Eden, that man fell. Problems in life always come from an unworthy desire in the heart. **"The**

heart is deceitful above all things and beyond cure. Who can understand it?" (Jeremiah 17:9). To be **pure** is to be without hypocrisy, which is the worst of all heart problems. It is a lie that has an attractive cover to hide the truth. It causes us to be dishonest, insincere and self-deceiving. The hypocrite may even claim a share in Christ and His righteousness. He might be involved in religious activity and appear to outdo the committed Christian. But God looks at the heart; He knows better. Judas confidently sat down with the apostles at Passover as if he were the holiest guest of all. Yet his heart was evil, and he went out and betrayed Christ.

A divided heart has always been a problem. One part of our being wants to know, worship, obey and please God. But because of our sinful nature another part wants to do its own thing. A pure heart in a person is shown by the degree to which the heart is less and less divided. Psalm 86:11 defines a pure heart: **"Teach me your way, O Lord, and I will walk in your truth; give me an undivided heart, that I may fear your name."**

The more **pure** our heart is, the more it will merge with God's will. Even when our best effort fails, the willing spirit of a pure heart means success to God.

SPIRITUAL CHARACTERISTIC NUMBER SEVEN
"Blessed are the peacemakers, for they will be called sons of God" (Matthew 5:9)

PEACEMAKERS

The history of mankind reflects that whatever ambitions a person may have, inner peace is one of the top priorities he strives to possess.

As members of the Kingdom of God, Christians are the only people who are able to give mankind the peace that everyone seeks. **"The fruit of the Spirit** [who lives within all who have been born again] **is love, joy, <u>peace</u>, patience, kindness, goodness, faithfulness, gentleness and self-control"** (Galatians 5:22-23a).

A peacemaker does not seek peace at any price; rather, a peacemaker has a different view because he is being delivered from concern for self. His interest is focused on bringing true inner peace to mankind regardless of personal sacrifice. He sees a much bigger and more important purpose in life. Jesus was the supreme example of this. He sacrificed His rights and went to the cross to bring peace to the hearts of mankind.

> SCRIPTURE THOROUGHLY CONDEMNS THE HUMANISTIC WAY OF BRINGING PEACE.

The blessing promised to a peacemaker is a great tribute. Jesus said that **"they will be called sons of God."** You know the saying, "like father, like son"? When the characteristic of peacemaking becomes part of our nature, we will truly be acting like a son of God. This once again demonstrates how different the Kingdom of God is from the kingdom of the world.

Nothing else in Scripture so thoroughly condemns the humanistic way of bringing peace as does the Sermon on the Mount. In the world's kingdom, mankind will always experience international tension, threats of war and discord among people. Self-centeredness, greed and lust will always show themselves. They are an inherent part of man's sinful nature. Therefore, man's way of bringing peace—by political, economic, and social means—does not work. The only way is to go to the heart. That is the theme of all of Jesus' teachings. We must be made new from the inside out.

SOME POINTS TO REMEMBER

These seven spiritual characteristics mark the unique differences between what is to govern our way of life under Christ, and that which marks the life of a non-Christian. They show us just how dependent we are on the power of the Holy Spirit within us, and how useless is the

<u>power of our flesh</u> in living out the life of Christ. The degree to which these characteristics are developed in us is not the criteria for our salvation, but they directly impact how successful we will be in fulfilling God's mission of being the **salt of the earth** and the **light of the world**.

We are in the world, but we are no longer members of its kingdom. Therefore, we are to separate ourselves from its standards. This is essential if we are to declare the wonderful deeds of Him who called us out of darkness. **"You are a chosen race, a royal priesthood, a holy nation, God's own people, that you may declare the wonderful deeds of him who called you out of darkness into his marvelous light"** (1 Peter 2:9).

THE CHRISTIAN AND PERSECUTION

After Jesus lists the seven spiritual characteristics of those in the Kingdom of God, the very next verse is **"Blessed are those who are persecuted <u>because of righteousness</u>, for theirs is the kingdom of heaven"** (Matthew 5:10). I believe Jesus put things in this order because as these characteristics become more a part of our character, this is how we can expect the world to react. Just as the world did not know how to handle Jesus because He dealt with matters of the heart, the same has been true throughout history regarding His close followers. Therefore, the response of the world system is to try to extinguish this bright light that illuminates their darkness.

Although most American Christians have been able to avoid persecution, there are growing indications that the safety and ease we have experienced could change in the coming years. Therefore, it is important we understand Jesus' comment.

WHAT DID JESUS MEAN?

Living the way Jesus describes in the Sermon on the Mount requires characteristics different from the normal make-up of mankind. Jesus does not say we may be persecuted for being <u>objectionable</u> or <u>difficult</u>. Nor does He say we may be persecuted because we are fanatical or standing up for certain political principles or being noble. People have made great sacrifices, given up careers, wealth, even their lives, and they may be thought of as heroes and are praised by the world. But Christianity is more than that! These things may not be wrong if we have that inclination, but they do not equal righteousness.

Jesus said, **"If the world hates you, keep in mind that it hated me first. If you belonged to the world, it would love you as its own. As it is, you do not belong to the world, but I have chosen you out of the world. That is why the world hates you. Remember the word I spoke to you: 'No servant is greater than his master.' If they persecuted me, they will persecute you also"** (John 15:18-20). Also, 2 Timothy 3:12 reads, **"In fact, everyone who wants to live a godly life in Christ Jesus will be persecuted."**

"Blessed are those who are persecuted because of righteousness." Practicing righteousness means being like Jesus Christ. Unfortunately, in the religious world, the meaning of righteousness often involves what can be done in the power of the flesh. But I strongly believe the righteousness He is talking about has more to do with matters of the heart.

From the days of the early church, through the Dark Ages and the Reformation, and unfortunately in all too many countries today, Christians have known terrible persecution. This is not because they have been difficult or overzealous, but only because they sought to live righteous lives. Some of the most grievous persecutions have been at the hands of an established religion. Those who persecuted Jesus, the early church, the Reformers, the Puritans, and other followers of Jesus through the ages often thought they were serving God. Formal Christianity has often been a great enemy of the pure faith.

WHY THE RIGHTEOUS ARE PERSECUTED

We might ask, why are the righteous persecuted while often the good and noble are not? There is something about the righteousness of Christ that convicts others. Christians don't have to condemn others; just the righteous way they live is enough to make some feel uneasy.

Therefore, they try to find fault. Being persecuted for righteousness really puts to the test our idea of what it means to be a Christian. Jesus said, **"Woe to you when all men speak well of you, for that is how their fathers treated the false prophets"** (Luke 6:26). We usually think the perfect Christian is the popular person who is easy to get along with. But the real Christian is probably not going to be praised by everybody.

True righteousness is developing and living the Christ life, represented by the characteristics Jesus gives us in the Beatitudes: to be poor in spirit regarding all natural abilities; to mourn for the sins we see in ourselves and in the

> # THE CHRISTIAN'S LIFE IS REFLECTIVE OF JESUS CHRIST.

world; to be meek in our relationships with others; to hunger and thirst for righteousness; to be merciful, which is to have pity for others <u>and</u> do something about it; to be pure in heart, honestly and without hypocrisy; to be a peacemaker. The message of the Sermon on the Mount is that we are becoming like Him. It also means we are becoming **salt** and **light** in a dark world. Because light exposes darkness and darkness hates the light, it brings persecution.

REJOICE AND BE GLAD WHEN PERSECUTED

Jesus continues by saying, **"Blessed are you when people insult you, persecute you and falsely say all kinds of evil against you because of me. <u>Rejoice and be glad</u>, because great is your reward in heaven, for in the same way they persecuted the prophets who were before you"** (Matthew 5:11-12). If the previous statement about persecution seemed challenging, this one is even more so. There are three principles that the Lord makes here in regard to the Christian.

One: The Christian is **unlike** everyone who is not a Christian. There is a light in the Christian's character that penetrates the spiritual darkness of a non-Christian's heart. Therefore, non-Christians tend to retaliate. They criticize, scorn, talk angrily about, speak evil of, abuse physically—socially—in the workplace and maybe even in the church.

Two: The Christian's life is reflective of Jesus Christ, and our concern is to do everything for His sake. Jesus says it is because we are living for Him that we are no longer like those of the world who live for themselves. This is why Christians are persecuted!

Three: <u>Our life is to be controlled by thoughts of Heaven.</u> The Old Testament saints were looking for a city whose builder and maker is God. Nothing that happened to them took their focus off the reward that was to come. How contrary this is to the motives that are in the world, always tempting us with an escape from reality with its pleasures and entertainment, especially avoiding thinking about death and the world to come.

How Christians Are to Face Persecution

There are many ways in which a Christian may suffer persecution, and the Bible tells us how we are to face it. **One,** the Christian is not to retaliate, even though our natural instinct is self-preservation and/or revenge. **Two,** we are not to feel resentment. This is very difficult, but judgment is to be left up to God. **Three,** we should not allow persecution to dishearten or oppress us.

I have sometimes experienced persecution because of my commitment to Christ. At first I did not have victory! I had to learn that this can only come through the power of the Holy Spirit living in me. Praise the Lord, He did provide that power, the heavy burden in my heart was lifted, and the fruit of the Spirit reigned once again in my heart.

It is difficult to relate to the subject of physical persecution unless one has personally experienced it. For example, have you ever wondered how the early Christians could sing while being fed to the lions? I remember reading the book *The Hiding Place*, about Corrie ten Boom's life. She asked her father if they could stand up under the persecution at the hands of the Germans. He responded by asking, "Corrie, when do you need a ticket to get on the train?" The answer, of course, is not until you are boarding the train. He was trying to help her understand that it is the same with the Lord. We won't need the Lord's strength, and He doesn't provide it, until it is needed.

Why would Jesus say we are to rejoice and be glad? One reason is because it is proof of what and who we are. It identifies us with the prophets, God's chosen servants, who are now with Him. Another reason is that it means our lives have become more like His. We are being treated as Jesus was, which again is proof that we belong to Him. We can also rejoice because Jesus says **our reward** in Heaven will be great. He is telling us that our ultimate destiny is fixed. If the world persecutes us, it just reminds us that we do not belong to it. We belong to another Kingdom, which is another good reason to rejoice!

After speaking about how we are to react to persecution, Jesus says, **"You are the light of the world. A city on a hill cannot be hidden. Neither do people light a lamp and put it under a bowl. Instead they put it on its stand, and it gives light to everyone in the house. In the same way, let your light shine before men, that they may see your good deeds and praise your Father in heaven"** (Matthew 5:14-16).

Having concluded our examination of God's special calling for America and the fundamentals of how He expects us to live in a world that does not know Him, we are ready to examine the nature of Satan's attack against us, and how we should respond.

QUESTIONS FOR GROUP DISCUSSION AND/OR TO BE ANSWERED INDIVIDUALLY

What are some of the personal characteristics that mark a typical person living by the standards of the kingdom of the world?

_____

_____

_____

_____

_____

What characteristics signify a person whom God is changing into a productive member of the Kingdom of God?

_____

_____

_____

_____

_____

_____

Why can't a person on his or her own just start behaving like a member of the Kingdom of God?

_____

_____

_____

_____

_____

_____

_____

The characteristic of mourning over sin—our own and those of the world—is not as evident in the church as it once was. Do you agree or disagree? Give reasons for your response.

_____

_____

_____

_____

_____

_____

What is it about the lifestyle of "Kingdom of God" living that often prompts strong opposition and persecution?

_____

_____

_____

_____

_____

_____

_____

Answer Christ's question: "When salt loses its saltiness, how can it be made salty again?"

_____

_____

_____

_____

_____

_____

CHAPTER SIX

A SPIRITUAL WAR ZONE

It was in the Garden of Eden that sin first entered God's creation. Throughout history Satan has repeatedly used this identical pattern of deception that he used against Adam and Eve. The same temptations we face and the choices we make every day are displayed for us in this tragic story.

As the account unfolds in Genesis, we notice that at first everything was good. There is no hint of rebellion. **"God saw all that He had made, and it was very good. And there was evening, and there was morning—the sixth day"** (Genesis 1:31). Here is a picture of perfect fellowship between God and His created beings. God and man walked together in happy communion.

God's Word to Adam and Eve was short and simple. **"'You are free to eat from any tree in the garden; but you must not eat from the tree of the knowledge of good and evil, for when you eat of it you will surely die'"** (Genesis 2:16,17). There was just one command to keep! You'd think it wouldn't be that hard!

SATAN CARES NOTHING ABOUT OUR SUFFERING.

Satan knew if he could cause Adam and Eve to exercise their independence and disobey, it would break the bonds of their fellowship, and God would lose something precious to Him. The enemy cared nothing about all the suffering that would follow.

To accomplish his goal, the devil employed several tactics. His methods remain basically the same to this day. **"Now the serpent [Satan] was more crafty than any of the wild animals the Lord God had made. He said to the woman, 'Did God really say, *You must not eat from any tree in the Garden*?' The woman said to the serpent, 'We may eat fruit from the trees in the garden, but God did say, *You must not eat from the tree that is in the middle of the garden, and you must not touch it, or you will die.*' 'You will not surely die,' the serpent said to the woman. 'For God knows that when you eat of it your eyes will be opened, and you will be like God, knowing good and evil.' When the woman saw that the fruit of the tree was good for food and pleasing to the eye, and was also desirable for gaining wisdom, she took some and ate it. She also gave some to her husband, who was with her, and he ate it"** (Genesis 3:1-6).

> SATAN USES ANYTHING AND EVERYTHING TO DRAW US AWAY FROM THE TRUTHS OF SCRIPTURE.

Satan's **first** attack technique was to plant a seed of doubt, and then outright deny the meaning of God's Word (Genesis 3:1-4).

We must be careful to stay alert, because it is easy for the enemy to influence us through the many avenues of the world. We are constantly being confronted with spiritual issues that challenge the standards of God as given in Scripture. The enemy will try to raise doubts in our minds about the importance of following God's Word. Satan will use anything and everything he can to draw us away from the truths of Scripture.

If we are not careful, we too will begin to rationalize situations in our minds. There will always be a temptation to serve our desires rather than remain obedient to what is taught in the Bible. Our subconscious plays tricks on us. *This can't really make that much difference to God.* Or, *God's Word doesn't actually mean this, does it?* Satan's next step is to turn the doubt into outright denial. *God understands; He doesn't mind. He wants me to have what I think is best.*

If we ignore God's Word, as Adam and Eve did, we too break our communion with God, and like them we will suffer spiritual defeat. Not only that, but the next time a similar situation occurs, it will be much easier for Satan to get us to fall again. Before long, our conscience has lost its sensitivity, and we no longer obey that particular standard. Doubt first, then denial. That's how Satan's deceptions work.

Please note that I am not talking about the times when we make a mistake and fall; we all make mistakes. And, of course, we all begin our Christian lives as spiritual babies. But God desires that we quickly mature as we grow in the knowledge of His Word and the workings of His Holy Spirit. As this happens, we come under conviction as the Spirit reminds us of the Word. But if the enemy gets us to a point where the Holy Spirit can no longer bring about conviction concerning something addressed in the Bible, we have fallen into deception. This will not necessarily happen immediately; this changing of our thinking can take place gradually.

Satan's next attack technique was to deceive Adam and Eve into elevating themselves, *to be like God,* so that they made their own decisions about right and wrong. **"When the woman saw that the fruit of the tree was good for food** [lust of the flesh] **and pleasing to the eye** [lust of the eyes]**, and also desirable for gaining wisdom** [pride of life]**, she took some and ate it"** (Genesis 3:6). Knowing what Eve had done, God said to her, **"'What is this you have done?' The woman said, 'The serpent deceived me, and I ate'"** (Genesis 3:13).

By tempting her to use human wisdom to decide right and wrong, Satan deceived Eve into rebelling against God's command. It is no different today. If we don't follow God's Word as our standard, by default we will accept the standards of society. However, this should not be true of those who have been reborn spiritually. Members of God's Kingdom look to Scripture to establish our standards of good and evil. We are no longer members of the kingdom of the world. This means, as 1 Peter 5:8 warns, that we must constantly be on the alert, because Satan will try to deceive us. He prowls around like a roaring lion looking for someone to devour.

Another point to observe is how freely Satan used the name of God. He didn't ask Eve to deny God or to quit walking with Him. In fact, he told her that following his advice would make her more like God. He just encouraged her to disregard God's Word, to doubt that God was serious about the one command He had given them.

When attacking through deception, Satan's temptations could reference the name of God or something that appears to be godly. But if the inner motivation is to serve the desires of our flesh, **be on guard**.

SATAN'S TEMPTATION OF JESUS

In similar fashion, Satan did not lure Jesus with the sensual vices of the world to deceive Him. Nor did he suggest that He deny God. He tempted our Lord with self-serving attractions. He encouraged Jesus to step out on His own, to become independent and make His own decisions rather than following the words of His Father.

It is worthy to note that just as Satan used "the lust of the flesh," "the lust of the eyes," and "the pride of life" to deceive Adam and Eve, he used these same three self-serving techniques in his attempt to deceive and cause Jesus to disobey the Word of God. This account is recorded in both Matthew (chapter 4:1-10) and Luke (chapter 4:1-12). Jesus answered all three temptations by what is written in Scripture.

Satan also tempted Jesus through a friend of His. In Matthew 16, Jesus had asked His disciples, **"'Who do you say I am?' Simon Peter answered, 'You are the Christ, the Son of the living God.' Jesus replied, '...this was not revealed to you by man, but by my Father in heaven'"** (Matthew 16:15-17). Peter had received a revelation from God. But notice what happened immediately following:

"From that time on Jesus began to explain to His disciples that He must go to Jerusalem and suffer many things at the hands of

the elders, chief priests and teachers of the law, and that he must be killed and on the third day be raised to life. Peter took him aside and began to rebuke him. 'Never, Lord!' he said. 'This shall never happen to you!' Jesus turned and said to Peter, 'Get behind me, Satan! You are a stumbling block to me; you do not have in mind the things of God, but the things of men'" (Matthew 16:21-23). Peter's motivating force was self-preservation for Jesus over and above the will of God.

Learning how Satan attempts to deceive us by using "the lust of the flesh," "the lust of the eyes," and "the pride of life" is an important biblical lesson. It is even more so in these last days as the world now has so many ways to tempt us in these three areas.

At various times we have all fallen victim to deception. And when we do, it can cause a multitude of personal problems and require that we understand another important biblical principle—repentance. We must quickly turn from what deceived us, and confess it to the Lord. Without repentance, our position of living in victory through the power of the Holy Spirit is seriously affected.

Two Major Warfronts

Have you ever stopped to consider that America is actually engaged in two major warfronts? You probably remember where you were on the morning of September 11, 2001, when millions of Americans huddled around their TV sets. The impossible happened that day, and we are still faced with threats of future terrorist attacks. Our country has entered into a major war against an enemy that has no conventional military and is of no specific nationality. It is a faceless foe.

But there is another fierce war being waged in our country that every Christian needs to be aware of. It is a life-and-death struggle with our spiritual adversary, Satan. He is out to destroy the spiritual heritage of our nation. The difference between the attacks of 9/11 and this second warfare is that the terrorist attack was obvious and abrupt. Because of this, the country united and took swift action! This second attack has slowly been taking place during the last 40-50 years, and tragically, Christians do <u>not</u> stand united in their response. How many believers do you know who talk about or even understand our country's second warfront? Both wars have the same objective—to destroy the foundation upon which America was built.

SPIRITUAL ATTACK AGAINST AMERICA

With what the Lord has taught me and I am sharing with you, I can say without hesitation that we are living in a crucial period of time. America is under a vicious attack from God's great enemy. Prophetic Scriptures warn us that this would happen. Unfortunately, Satan's success in the last few decades has been overwhelming.

This spiritual warfare began in earnest after World War II—after America became the greatest superpower in the history of mankind. That is when the moral standards that had bound our nation together for generations began to unravel. Deception has been at the root of the enemy's attacks.

We can readily see the effect of this spiritual encounter on our American society. But Satan's main opponent is not society at large, but the Body of Christ. The devil is always scheming to dilute our saltiness, to keep us from preserving the good and dim our light in a dark world.

A SPIRITUAL WAR ZONE

It is well-known that for some time America has been a great center of Christianity. This means that if we accept what the Scriptures teach about Satan, a major thrust of his spiritual warfare in these last days will be in our country. Understanding this is key to knowing where Satan's major spiritual battleground will be in the last days. Satan has always tried to sabotage any work of God by undermining what God is doing.

Therefore, as Satan sees his time growing short, he will try to destroy every good thing with which God has blessed our country, especially our Christian values. It also means that many of the prophetic warnings given in Scripture about the last days apply to America as much as anywhere else, if not more so.

The U.S. has indeed become a major spiritual war zone. We are being hit in every way imaginable to compromise biblical standards. Many Christians readily admit they do not understand the root cause of the rapid breakdown in our society's moral fiber, or the methods by which the enemy has conducted such a successful campaign. This has obviously taken its toll on the effectiveness of the body of Christ to fulfill our mission to be salt and light. These 'new moral' standards have influenced the Christian community much more than we have influenced the world. We have become more tolerant to the sins of the world, while this generation feels free to promote its sins, not only by their lifestyle, but also through the media that is available to everyone. This was not the case throughout most of America's history.

> SATAN HAS ALWAYS WORKED TO SABOTAGE GOD'S PURPOSE.

SATAN'S PAST ATTACKS

God and His people have always had a spiritual enemy, and any work of the Lord involves spiritual battles. The fact that the devil is out to destroy God's calling for Christians in our land is not unique. He has always worked to sabotage God's purpose. His tactics are ruthless and deadly. He never calls for a spiritual cease-fire!

In the days of Noah, he caused lawlessness to become so terrible that God had no choice but to cleanse the Earth by a flood. As you read through the Old Testament you discover that the devil was constantly developing a spirit of permissiveness and rebellion in Israel. When God Himself came to Earth in the person of Jesus Christ, Satan had so deceived most of the Israelites, they not only didn't recognize Him, they crucified Him.

Satan's warfare against God's people continued after the church began. In the first 300 years of church history, Satan's attacks against

Christians, worked primarily through the Roman government, were so harsh that an estimated three million Christians were persecuted by every cruel act of torture imaginable. They were thrown to wild animals, torn to pieces, beheaded, burned, buried alive and crucified.

Satan's attacks on the church continued during the Dark Ages and the Middle Ages. Much of the church operated in secret during these time periods. After Martin Luther posted his *Ninety-Five Theses* on the doors of the Castle Church in Wittenberg, Germany on October 31, 1517, the Reformation began, and the Gospel of Jesus Christ started to be preached openly. Satan, however, continued his attacks against Christians, and thousands were brutally massacred for their faith.

> DECEPTION IS
> DESTROYING THE
> MORAL STANDARDS
> OF AMERICAN
> CHRISTIANS.

In France in 1557, the Pope called for an extermination of all believers who were not members of the Roman Catholic Church. On August 24, 1572, 70,000 Christians were killed in the St. Bartholomew's Day massacre. The Spanish Inquisition left more than 100,000 people dead and 1,500,000 banished from the country. Between 1566 and 1598, some 100,000 born-again Christians were slaughtered in the Netherlands. In the country of Bohemia, 3,200,000 Christians were exterminated during the Reformation Wars. And persecution of the church continues. Historian David Barrett estimates that more than **45 million** Christians were martyred during the 20th century, including 13,300,000 since 1950.

For the most part, America has enjoyed freedom from religious persecution, and remains a center of Christian witness for the world. Thus, from what the Scriptures teach and from what history has confirmed, it is easy to see why Satan has launched an all-out spiritual attack against our country. He is doing all he can to change every law based on Christian standards. The American church must be aware of this.

There is no doubt that we are living in a time of his attack. Prophetic Scriptures warn us that this will happen.

PERSECUTION AND DECEPTION

The Bible teaches that Satan has always used two distinct methods when attacking God's people: **persecution and deception!** Both have the same goal—to keep God's people from fulfilling their mission of being the **salt of the earth** and the **light of the world**. Persecution is easy to detect; deception is not. We can clearly see how Satan uses persecution. He uses deception just as much, if not more so, but it is harder to verify.

Persecution is an attack that usually causes physical harm. Satan's objective is to get us to deny our relationship with Jesus in order to avoid persecution. Look at the lives of the apostles, almost all of whom were martyred for their faith. Consider this thought from someone who recently experienced persecution and was asked why God had allowed it: *"Not only would He not kill our enemies for us, but He would empower us to love them while they killed us."*

DECEPTION

Both persecution and deception are dangerous and destructive. However, deception has been the primary method of attack against Christians in America. Deception tempts our sinful nature (using the lust of the eyes, the lust of the flesh, and the pride of life) to disobey God's Word. This is my definition of deception: *Seducing spirits tempt God's people to exchange the truth of God's Word for that which is contrary to the Word of God. They attempt to make something wrong seem innocent and irresistible. They try to make the difference between black and white seem like a shade of gray.*

If we do not know the Word of God and diligently seek righteousness, and hate every evil way, we will become susceptible to these deceiving spirits. The Apostle Paul writes, **"The Spirit clearly says that in later times some will abandon the faith and follow deceiving spirits"**

(I Timothy 4:1). Deception is insidious and dangerous. **It breeds compromise, which leads to disobedience and spiritual defeat!** The only way to determine the use of deception is by an examination of the fruit. As we look at the fruit produced by our society in this last generation, keep in mind that **"the fruit of the Spirit is love, joy, peace, patience, kindness, goodness, faithfulness, gentleness and self-control"** (Galatians 5:22-23).

Through persecution, some 70 million Christians have been killed over the last 2000 years (source: *World Christian Encyclopedia*, Global Diagram 6). But Satan's use of deception is also ruthless, wicked and severe. It brought down Eve, then Adam, as well as leaders like Samson, Saul, David and Solomon. Today it is destroying the moral standards of American Christians. Many church members and leaders have fallen into sin through deception.

One of the strongest influences the world has had on the Christian community has been to make us self-centered. A fruit of spiritual deception is to serve our self-interests over and above our desire to please God and put His standards first. We may say we are standing against the tide, but in truth, we are simply a few decades behind the world's acceptance of many of our society's 'new moral standards.' What was permissible twenty or thirty years ago by the world is now acceptable by many Christians. Finding a Christian who has a <u>fear of sinning</u> is rare these days.

FRUIT REVEALS DECEPTION

In this past generation, Americans have changed the way we raise our families, teach in our schools, run our government and establish our social order. America's 'new' moral code says, "If you can get away with it, it's all right." Personal accountability, respect for authority and self-control have become an antiquated way of thinking. Nothing, it seems, is repugnant or indecent. Very little deserves to be honored and respected as rules and boundaries are fought against. Actions which were "unthinkable" thirty-to-forty years ago have become "commonplace."

Even our government leaders have passed legislation that has allowed for immoral causes and ungodly standards. Passing out condoms in schools, for example, sanctions promiscuity. School prayer was made illegal. A law was passed that has allowed the murder of more than 50 million innocent babies through abortion.

A report that covered a recent 30-year period showed the bad fruit our society has produced. Crime increased by 500%, illegitimate births by 400%! Three times the number of children were living in single-parent homes. The teenage suicide rate

COMMITMENT TO FAMILY HAS BEEN SHATTERED.

tripled. The divorce rate doubled. It became OK for schools to teach homosexuality as an acceptable lifestyle. The entertainment industry discovered it could display sexual permissiveness and violence with little resistance. Child molestation and incest became a national disaster, with police stating that only 25% of all cases are reported. Our children began to gun down peers and teachers at school. Every day the newspapers are filled with reports of robbery, rape, murder, greed, gang violence and other horrors.

In American society today, the most fundamental means of preserving social order—commitment to family—has been shattered. Unethical conduct and greed have tainted such professions as doctors, bankers, lawyers, politicians, educators, corporate leaders and even spiritual leaders, who historically have been the pillars of our society. Our great American cities, once the principle evidence of a mighty industrial nation, have become a stalking ground for crime, violence, sexual perversion and drugs. The character of many Americans has also transformed through sexual immorality into a lifestyle devoted to self-gratification. By passing laws that actively undermine the truth, our great republic form of government has turned from the scriptural principles that formed the foundation of our country.

Humanistic philosophy has captured public education! Public school textbooks no longer teach the Christian influence in our country's development. However, nearly every book has the religion of humanism running through its pages. It is a religion that teaches the perfection of human ideas about right verses wrong and the development of culture to be mankind's guide, not God and His Word. This is definitely one of the reasons why our Christian heritage, which burned brightly for many generations, has been extinguished so quickly. We are seeing what Abraham Lincoln said come true: *"The philosophy of the classroom today will be the philosophy of the government tomorrow."*

Let me site just one fruit in our public schools of many that have been produced by this humanistic religion that is being taught throughout our society. A survey completed by Gospel Films reported that in 1940 the major discipline problems in public schools were: Talking in class, chewing gum, making noise, running in the halls, cutting in line, improper clothing and littering. One generation later in 1983 the major discipline problems were: Rape, robbery, assault, burglary, arson, bombing and murder.

Dr. James Dobson, founder and president of Focus on the Family, and Gary L. Bauer, president of the Family Research Council wrote *Children at Risk*, a book detailing the battle in our society for the hearts and minds of our kids. Every parent and grandparent needs this kind of information and more. Speaking about our culture, they write: *"The same twisted philosophy that permits us to kill infants through abortion with impunity is now prevalent throughout the western world. This new way of thinking has produced a society that is extremely dangerous to minds and bodies of children* (emphasis added).

"At the arrival of adolescence, teenagers are subject to the pressure and wrath of their peers, making them prime targets for brainwashing with the mind-bending process at which television and movies constantly hammer away at moral values and principles. Any form of self-discipline or restraint is usually ridiculed by friends and acquaintances. This develops a lot of pressure for conformity, until finally, many of our youth trade in their freedom

for slavery and domination. Their behavior has been warped by the enormous social pressures coming through society. This opens the doors of temptation which carry many names: alcohol, marijuana, hard drugs, pornography, gambling, homosexual experimentation, premarital sex and more.

"It should be clear that one of our jobs as parents must be to keep these temptation doors closed, locked and barred to adolescents. It is frightening today to see that these doors are not only unlocked for many of our youth— they are wide open. It is no wonder that the kids who want to remain chaste are often made to feel like prudes and freaks.

"With the heartache and illness the loose humanistic standards are now causing for the families of our society, one would think responsible adults would be united in a campaign in opposition. But normally the contrary is found to be true."

Does it concern you that the moral standard by which the American people lived for years has deteriorated more in this last generation than in all of the years combined since we became a nation? It is not pleasant to con-

THE MAJORITY OF PEOPLE IGNORE THE SCOREBOARD!

sider these truths. I would rather hear about the positives than the negatives. But when you are in a battle, you cannot afford to hide your head in the sand or you will soon face defeat. The spiritual foundation of our country is being eroded. Yet the majority of people, including Christians, do not seem all that concerned. They ignore the scoreboard!

FULFILLING OUR MISSION STATEMENT

We need look no further than ourselves to find the real reason behind the corruption and violence in our nation. As the cartoon character Pogo said, "We have met the enemy, and he is us!" It is imperative that Christians see clearly how Satan's work of deception is bringing this great country to the brink of destruction. The Body of Christ has lost much of its light and the function of being salt. We have allowed society to exchange our commitment to righteousness for a spirit of tolerance toward the ways of the world.

The principle of Jesus' teaching is that if Christians assimilate anything other than the purity of God's Word, we will become contaminated and lose our saltiness. Our influence on society is dependent upon our being distinct from the world, not identical to it. Herein lies the problem. This is the reason for the bitter harvest of suffering and defeat. **"But you have planted wickedness, you have reaped evil, you have eaten the fruit of deception. Because you have depended on your own strength"** (Hosea 10:13).

When talking about deception I am reminded of the story about a frog. The frog was put into a pan of cold water. The water was then slowly heated so that the frog didn't notice the water becoming warm. As the water continues to heat to a boil, the frog is gradually overcome and never legitimately tries to escape. He didn't become alarmed because the change was not sudden. Therefore, he paid little attention to what was happening. The results were he became a casualty to his environment by being overcome by deception.

The fruit of our society compared to the teachings of Jesus Christ is not a pretty picture. However, we cannot blame the people of the world. The people of the world will naturally do what the standards of the society in which they live allow. They are part of the kingdom of the world. They live in darkness! But <u>we</u> know better, and that is why Jesus declared that it is our responsibility to be salt and light. Are you one who has been slowly caught in the web of deception by the changes that have been taking place in our society the past 40-50 years?

QUESTIONS FOR GROUP DISCUSSION AND/OR TO BE ANSWERED INDIVIDUALLY

How seriously do you sense that your Christian friends take the devil?

_____

_____

_____

_____

_____

_____

_____

Contrast Satan's two techniques of deception and persecution by listing what he might see as the advantages and disadvantages of each.

_____

_____

_____

_____

_____

_____

_____

Name some influences that have made today's American Christians more susceptible to the deceptions of the devil.

_____

_____

_____

_____

_____

_____

_____

What do you think it will take to bring the American church to a greater awareness of the intense spiritual warfare going on?

_____

_____

_____

_____

_____

_____

Do you foresee the persecution of Christians ever being practiced in the United States? Why or why not?

_____

_____

_____

_____

_____

_____

On a scale of one to ten, 10 being the best, give today's American church a "salt and light" rating.

_____

_____

_____

_____

_____

_____

CHAPTER SEVEN

DECEPTION ILLUSTRATED

DECEPTION ILLUSTRATED THROUGH THE STORY OF AN EAGLE

The eagle is an amazing example of God's creation. This bird is mentioned more than 30 times in Scripture. Eagles are swift, having been clocked at up to 150 miles per hour in flight. Their powerful seven-foot wing span allows them to glide effortlessly at heights up to one-half mile, and the aerodynamics of their wing construction permits flight even in hurricane-force winds. The eagle's eye has two fovea (areas of acute vision), from which they can spot prey two miles away. With their amazing depth perception they can dive accurately at speeds of up to 200 miles per hour.

Due to a bony protrusion that extends outward over the eyelid, the eagle's appearance is decidedly different from that of other birds. This stern expression gives the eagle an air of royalty. Its grandeur and grace have been revered for centuries. It has been the symbol of some of the world's greatest countries and leaders including America.

Picture this monarch of the sky perched high on a mountain ledge overlooking a valley with a beautiful stream far below. Basking in the morning sun, surveying his domain, the eagle launches himself into the air. He sails over the green valley and swoops down toward the stream, heading for his favorite fishing spot to catch his breakfast.

When he arrives at the stream's bank, his keen eyes notice something is slightly different. There is a large rock near his fishing spot.

He knows this rock has never been there before, so he flies by the area without stopping and perches on the limb of a nearby tree. He wants to determine whether this new object is dangerous. He sits watching for better than an hour, looking up and down the stream. There is no activity whatsoever, so he drops down and lands on the rock.

In the nearby grass is a large fish. He is drawn to it, but he is puzzled. The fish is not near the stream; it is several feet from the shore. The eagle is suspicious. Something isn't right. He scans the grassy area, the nearby bushes, and the shore of the mountain stream. There seems to be no danger, so he jumps off the rock, clutches the fish in his talons and is about to fly away when he notices another fish close by in the grass. Then another! The wilderness is providing for him in a most unusual way this morning!

> THE EAGLE DEVELOPED A MIND OF ACCEPTANCE.

Hiding in the thicket on the other side of the stream, a trapper is watching the bird's every move. This hunter has been promised a large sum of money to capture an eagle alive. And he knows this will require his craftiest skills.

The next day, the eagle returns to his fishing spot. The rock is still there. He again observes the area from the nearby tree—but this time for only a few minutes. More quickly satisfied that no danger exists, he flies to the rock again. Lo and behold, the supply of fish has been miraculously replenished. This is unbelievable! Mother Nature is providing for him in a marvelous way, giving him more time to soar through the heavens, viewing his lovely mountain domain.

Several days pass, and the eagle is becoming conditioned. Now each morning he goes directly to the rock. Each day he finds fish there. He jumps down from the rock, grabs a fish and jumps back on the rock to enjoy his meal. He loves it! This is saving him a lot of time, which can now be used for other activities. The eagle has developed a mind of acceptance. The trapper is ready for his next move.

He makes a strong hoop like a fish net about four feet in diameter. To this he attaches a long handle with a curved bow. The next night he goes to the mountain stream where he first placed the rock and carefully digs into the ground at the base of the rock, positioning the handle of the net in the ground at an angle. This allowed the hoop to hover about three feet above the rock, yet the bow keeps the net fairly level. Then, as he has been doing every night, he places fresh fish in the nearby grass.

The next morning, the eagle perches on his lofty lookout as usual, enjoying the beauty of his surroundings. In about an hour, he lifts off and begins what has become a leisurely flight to his favorite spot. The eagle's assumption that nature is providing his food is developing in him a somewhat sluggish disposition. As the eagle draws near the rock, he is suddenly troubled. There is an odd structure erected above it. He checks his flight and begins to soar in circles. He flies fairly high, trying to make out this strange object. He can see the fish are there as usual. After 20 minutes of flight, he senses no danger, so he descends and lands on a nearby treetop. There he spends an hour in complete silence, listening intently and watching for any strange movement. There is nothing!

A good 200 yards away, however, hidden in the thick bushes, is the clever trapper, patiently watching every move the great bird makes. Eventually the eagle flies down to the shore, landing away from the net. He finds a fish in the grass, eats it and grabs another and flies back to his nest. In the process, it appears that the strange object over the rock is probably harmless.

That afternoon, as the eagle is soaring high above the valley, he can't erase from his mind that new object over the rock. He has to know if it will interfere with the beautiful way his food is being provided. After circling it several times, he flies back to the rock and lands on the handle of the net. Nothing happens!

There are still a couple of fish near the rock ... under the net. He hops down to test this strange structure. He reaches out with his beak and claw clutching one of the fish and then quickly hops back. The net doesn't move.

For the next few days the eagle proceeds with caution. With each visit he surveys the area closely, making certain there is nothing else new. He moves quickly, devouring one fish and carrying a second to his nest, all the time staying away from the rock. As time passes, he regains his confidence that all is well. Once again he begins to take a fish and perch on the rock, which is directly under the net, to enjoy his banquet.

The trapper is now ready. Before dawn the next morning, he adjusts the arrangement of the net. He ties a strong cord to the rim of the hoop. He runs the cord down to the ground by the rock, under a small root, and into the thick bushes nearby. To test the cord, he pulls on it, bending the rim of the net down until it covers the rock. Finally he baits the trap with the usual fish. All is ready. Then he moves into the nearby thicket to wait in quiet anticipation.

Right on time, the eagle returns the next morning. Though intelligent, he has been deceived into accepting this strange element and free fish as part of the established order. He lands on the sand near the rock, grabs a fish and perches on the stone under the net to enjoy his meal. At that exact moment, the eagle senses a slight movement in the thicket. His muscles tighten! He is ready to spring into the safety of the air, but before he can move, the four-foot hoop with the net attached comes down over him with a swish.

There is an intense battle—the eagle against the net. Beating his wings, tearing at the net with his beak, he fights for his freedom. He strains with every ounce of energy, but eventually the great bird is helpless. The mighty and glorious monarch of the sky has fallen to defeat <u>through deception</u>.

This short story illustrates several principles of deception that we should all be aware of. Most of Satan's deceptive traps are hidden, but there is usually some sign of their presence. We are warned, **"Dear friends, do not believe every spirit, but test the spirits to see whether they are from God, because many false prophets** [teachers] **have gone out into**

the world" (1 John 4:1). The most reliable way to test the spirits is to search the Scriptures. What we are tempted to accept must be in compliance with the spiritual principles in God's Word. This should be done with prayer and a time of cautious waiting to make sure our emotions are no longer the determinate part of any decisions we make. Remember, we still have the sinful nature we were born with, which is self-centered. As Jesus used the Word of God to combat the temptations of the enemy (see Matthew 4:1-11), we are to follow His example and act in the same way.

The eagle ignored his instincts. Adam and Eve were lured into deception by what they saw with their eyes—the lust of the eyes—rather than obeying God's instruction. The eagle was drawn to the trap through an appeal to one of his basic needs. Satan's deadly temptations always include an appeal—lust of the flesh—to a basic need or want, such as food, material possessions, security, acceptance, money, power, sex drive or beauty. These things are not inherently wrong, but satisfying these needs outside of God's plans is.

> THE EAGLE'S PRIDE MADE HIM BELIEVE HE HAD ALL THINGS UNDER CONTROL.

The eagle had inner warnings of the hidden dangers, but his desires caused him to act against his instincts. God provides us with warnings of spiritual danger. Like Jesus, we must by faith follow His Word instead of our wants and desires. It was the eagle's pride—the pride of life—that made him believe he had all things under control. Over time he became dull and sluggish, and eventually this cost him his freedom.

It is easy to let our guard down. One of Satan's most successful deceptions in this last generation has been how he has changed our attitude toward the sacred Scriptures and our failure to take them seriously. This is the exact opposite of the attitude Jesus had. The Bible is our textbook and our authority. We cannot rely solely upon subjective experiences, because there are evil spirits as well as good spirits. The Bible warns there are deceiving spirits that can cause us to have counterfeit experiences. The Scriptures teach that this will especially be true in the last days.

A current example of this is the dangerous way the church is teaching the relationship between law and grace. To say that because we are under grace we have nothing to do with law and can forget it, is definitely not what Scripture teaches, nor was this the attitude of Jesus. The law is not a means for salvation, but we are not to ignore it. We are to use it as our guide in living out our lives on this Earth as members of the Kingdom of God. **"The law of the Lord is perfect, reviving the soul. The statutes of the Lord are trustworthy, making wise the simple. The precepts of the Lord are right, giving joy to the heart. The commands of the Lord are radiant, giving light to the eyes. The fear of the Lord is pure, enduring forever. The ordinances of the Lord are sure and altogether righteous. They are more precious than gold, than much pure gold; they are sweeter than honey, than honey from the comb. By them is your servant warned; in keeping them there is great reward"** (Psalm 19:7-11).

The eagle became conditioned to his surroundings because he wanted to satisfy his desire for food. Though these new conditions were contrary to the laws of nature, the eagle accepted them because they allowed him more time for pleasure. Likewise, God's Word warns us, Satan will attempt to trick us into changing biblical standards through "self-serving" traps. Throughout history Satan has proven a master at tempting God's people with the advantages of sin, without revealing the pain they will surely suffer.

I also want to illustrate Satan's use of deception through the written testimony of my brother, Dr. Charles Fraley, M.D. He had a special calling of God on his life, but even though he was a dedicated Christian, he too was led into deception by the enemy.

DR. CHARLES FRALEY'S TESTIMONY

I was raised on a small farm near Greenville, Ohio, in a family of 13 children. I was number 12. My parents were godly people, sincerely dedicated to serving the Lord. Precept and example trained their children. Many who knew my mother testify to her exemplary Christian life, much like the outstanding women described in Proverbs 31.

Growing up, I had a strong desire to know the Lord. When I was seven, I joined the church and was baptized in a local creek, thinking this might help me go to Heaven. At age 11, I heard and understood the Gospel of Jesus Christ for the first time. I came under conviction for three days and nights until I finally made the decision to accept Jesus as Lord and Savior.

Upon graduating from high school, I entered the Navy. Our country was in the Korean War, and I was sure I would be drafted. This was a time of testing for me as I felt like one of the few committed Christians in the military.

While in the Navy, the Lord gave me a great desire to know Him better through His Word. I had spare time while on ship duty and spent most of those hours learning the Word of God. As a normal practice, I would rise two hours before wakeup call to pray, study the Bible and memorize Scripture. By the time my four-year tour of duty was over, I had memorized more than 800 verses, and would review about 150 of them every day from morning to night.

It was during my military service that I had a unique, or "supernatural," experience that led me to commit my life to the Lord's service. The presence of God surrounded me as I was reading Hebrews 13:5. The Lord spoke this verse to my spirit: **"Let your conversation be without covetousness; and be content with such things as you have: for He hath said, I will never leave thee, nor forsake thee"** (KJV). This caused me to commit my life into the Lord's hands and give up any plans of my own.

AFTER THE MILITARY

After military service, I felt led to enter Nyack Bible College in New York, supported by the GI Bill. It was there I met Marlene, the girl I would marry.

A few months into Bible College, I asked God what He wanted me to do with my life. As yet I had not received any clear directive. My prayer was quickly followed by a vision. Before I go on, let me explain that according to the Bible it is not unscriptural for the Lord to direct Christians through a vision or dream; however, to be sure it is of the Lord, any vision must be tested by examining whether it fits all of the principles found in Scripture. In the vision I saw a man standing over the ocean, with one foot in Africa and the other in America. He was dressed in doctor's clothing and saying, *"Come over and help, come over and help."* This call was somewhat similar to the Macedonian call the Apostle Paul experienced. As I sought the Lord for the meaning, the Spirit convicted me that I was to become a doctor and go to Africa to help the needy.

> I HAD GRADUALLY FALLEN INTO DECEPTION, THOUGH I HAD NOT REALIZED IT.

At that time I had never thought about being a doctor. I was not even familiar with medicine or healthcare. Growing up on a small farm in southwestern Ohio, I had never been academically inclined. My career plans were to be a farmer. The Lord blessed me with the faith to step out and transfer to Taylor University, a Christian liberal-arts university, where I entered pre-medical school. In the three years of pre-med, I was blessed with A's in nearly all of my classes.

I then went to medical school for four years at Ohio State, graduated, and served one year of internship and four years of surgical residency at Saint Elisabeth Hospital in Youngstown, Ohio. I passed the national exams of the American Board of Surgery and became a fully Board Certified General Surgeon. I had spent 13 years preparing myself so I could be obedient to the Lord's call to go to Africa as a missionary doctor.

However, during this period of preparation I had slipped in my spiritual walk. I had allowed thoughts to enter my mind, such as rationalizing that I could just as well serve the Lord by practicing medicine here in the States. That would allow me, along with my wife and the two children we now had, to enjoy all the benefits available to doctors in this country. Besides, I thought, if I ever did go to Africa, it would be good to have some practical experience beforehand. Several doctor friends and other Christians agreed.

The truth is, I had gradually <u>fallen into *deception*</u>, though I had not realized it. How did that happen? It is hard to say. It seemed to develop subtly over a period of time, and just infiltrated my mind. I justified it with the idea that I would still be willing to go overseas when the Lord showed me that I should. But the fact of the matter was, I had already received a direct leading from God to go to Africa.

MEDICAL PRACTICE

I started a practice in the area where I grew up. Soon I was earning a net income of up to $400,000 per year, and that was in the early 1970s. I had my own airplane and the best Buick you could buy. I bought the 100-acre family farm where most of my brothers and sisters had grown up and fixed it up with tractors, a pick-up truck, animals and horses. I was able to buy everything anyone in my family wanted, and it was all paid for.

My medical practice was successful; however, there was one major thing wrong. I was walking in disobedience to God's original call, which was to go to the mission field. Without even knowing it, I had fallen prey to the influence of the world.

The worst was yet to come! By being out of the Lord's will for my life, this opened the door for me to fall into an even greater *deception*. It happened about four years after I started my medical practice. In consideration of others, I won't go into the details. But it could have devastated not only me, but destroyed everything I had, including my family. Of course that is what Satan wanted! As Eve was *deceived* to eat the fruit from the Garden, I can also say: *"The enemy deceived me."*

A LESSON TO BE LEARNED

I am going to digress for a moment because there is an important lesson that anyone who claims to be a Christian can learn from my experience.

Although God is merciful and long-suffering, there comes a time when He expects us to clean up our lives, and the sooner the better! Otherwise, He will have to do it for us, which may require walking through some deep valleys that we will not like.

As a physician, I often had to assist Christians, including pastors and religious leaders, with personal problems. These are usually matters they do not want to share with others. Often it is secret sins that trip us up. It takes a humble Christian to admit he has a problem and to seek help. This is partly because many are too proud to admit they <u>have</u> a spiritual problem. When God says we are to come out of the ways of the world and be separate, He means that and for good reason. **"What agreement is there between the temple of God and idols? For we are the temple of the living God. As God has said: 'I will live with them and walk among them, and I will be their God, and they will be my people.' 'Therefore come out from them and be separate, says the Lord. Touch no unclean thing, and I will receive you.' 'I will be a Father to you, and you will be my sons and daughters, says the Lord Almighty.' Since we have these promises, dear friends, let us purify ourselves from everything that contaminates body and spirit, perfecting holiness out of reverence for God"** (2 Corinthians 6:16-7:1).

SPIRITUAL DEFEAT

I had been *deceived* by the enemy and fallen prey to worldly attractions. To deliver me from this, the Lord opened my spiritual eyes. When He did, I realized I had been walking in disobedience since finishing medical school. <u>I was devastated</u>. From my youth I had always had such a strong desire to serve the Lord.

I could not believe I had gotten so far out of the Lord's will. But it happened! I had been active in church during this time. I had studied the Word of God and spent time in prayer, but my disobedience to a direct command from the Lord allowed the enemy to *deceive* me. After realizing I had fallen into *deception*, I began to seek the Lord with all my strength and with a true heart of repentance. I sought the Lord for a new filling of the Holy Spirit and the power to walk with Him according to His will as I had once experienced. I put forth every ounce of my being seeking God for *seven* months, studying the Word, meditating, praying and worshiping Him in a state of repentance. I also sought the Lord in regard to why so many Christians seemed to be living such defeated lives.

At the end of this time, my family and I went on a vacation. I had decided to spend this time fasting and praying—seeking the Lord—still in a spirit of repentance. I was determined not to stop until I knew that the fullness of the Holy Spirit had once again been released in my being. Halfway through the second week of our vacation, I awoke one night and knew the presence of the Lord was in the room with me. I began to have visions similar to the one when the Lord called me to become a doctor.

A "BEAST" HOVERING OVER AMERICA WAS DEVOURING CHRISTIANS.

The first vision was that of a large head of a "beast" hovering over America. It was devouring Christians almost at will. The Spirit of the Lord showed me that this beast represented the power of materialism and pleasure in our country. It was swallowing up Christians by spiritually *deceiving* and then overcoming them through the influence of the materialistic and pleasure-seeking lifestyles that had developed in our society. Those Christians who were being overcome were hardly aware of what was happening.

I was convicted that this is what the enemy used to tempt, *deceive* and then conquer me in my spiritual walk. It was why so many had become apathetic toward the deterioration of the biblical standards in our country. This was also why numerous Christian families were experiencing major defeats, with thousands suffering hurt and pain.

I want to make clear that the Lord did not show me that it is wrong to have material things or enjoy wholesome pleasure. Rather, what He revealed to me was how the enemy is using our society to create an abnormal desire for material things and pleasure. He knows that if Christians become over-committed to everyday affairs, we will lose our spiritual discernment. We will no longer function as **the salt of the earth** and **the light of the world**, which we are called to be. Many of us fail to see that we are in the middle of a spiritual war that has produced self-centered, self-serving people. The attitude of the heart is the focus of God's warning through this vision. The commitment of Christians to satisfying their everyday wants has taken precedence over their commitment to obey God's standards. This is the sin that is taking us out from under the hedge of God's protection and is diluting the power of the Holy Spirit in our lives. One of Satan's most powerful tools in these last days to implant worldly standards in our minds has been the media—television, movies, press, Internet, etc., something the Christian community has never had to contend with.

That first vision of a beast hovering over America, attacking Christians, was confirmed by the Holy Spirit giving me several other visions of Jesus Christ. The Scriptures tell us the Holy Spirit always testifies of Jesus. In these I was shown how Jesus was willing to pay a tremendous price by going to the cross for the salvation of mankind. He was a disciplined person who would let nothing deter Him from His call. I was also shown the great love Jesus has for mankind, and that He was standing at the door of my heart, knocking, wanting to come in and re-establish the Lord's will in my life.

All of these visions had a profound impact on me. Through them the Holy Spirit was showing me what had caused my *deception*, and that Jesus did not deserve the kind of treatment I had given Him. I could now see how I had become neglectful, disobedient and unfaithful. Through *deception* the enemy had me on a path of falling away from living a biblically based Christian life.

Since the time of these visions, I have walked with a certain *holy fear* that has helped me follow His commandments. I consider it a great privilege to do so. It actually resulted in my following through with the

Lord's first directive to serve the people in Africa, which has been very joyful. My wife and I first went to Tanzania for a year and then to Kenya, where we served for 29 years. I recently was required to retire from the mission field as I had reached the age of 70.

These spiritual teachings about *deception* that came from the visions the Lord gave me must be taken seriously. If we are not alert and ready—if we have become slothful in our commitment—we could be in for a big surprise as the events of these last days unfold. Not only that, but we may already be caught in the web of *deception*. The majority of Christians in America are not prepared to stand against the spiritual attacks that are taking place daily to control the hearts and minds of American people.

There is no greater privilege than to know and serve Jesus. He paid a tremendous price for our salvation and has every right to expect that we would seek to fulfill the directive given to us in Romans 12:1-2. It reads, **"Therefore, I urge you, brothers, in view of God's mercy, to offer your bodies as living sacrifices, holy and pleasing to God— which is your spiritual worship. Do not conform any longer to the pattern of this world, but be transformed by the renewing of your mind. Then you will be able to test and approve what God's will is—his good, pleasing and perfect will."**

DR. FRALEY'S MINISTRY

This concludes my brother's testimony. Before I move on, however, I want to add the following about how the Lord used him in Africa after his repentance and restoration. It's a thrilling follow-up.

Dr. Charles Fraley, M.D., and his wife, Marlene, R.N., served the Lord on the mission field in Africa for 30 years. He became the medical coordinator & executive director of a large health ministry in Kenya. His list of responsibilities was almost endless. He and his wife shared the love of Christ as he oversaw five hospitals and established more than 50 health centers and dispensaries throughout the country.

Dr. Fraley delivered supplies, checked on patients and performed surgery. He assisted in administration, teaching of staff and encouraging each facility. His duties required him to spend many days away from home, traveling dirt, rock and sand roads. He also faced risk from African tribes and wild animals, which sometimes posed life-threatening dangers. In addition, when he went into the bush country, he lived as the natives, eating their food, and often sleeping in his vehicle or under the stars.

He and his wife were involved in building a new hospital and establishing a nursing school on one of the largest mission stations of its kind in the world—the African Inland Mission Station in Kijabe, Kenya. It provides some of the highest-quality healthcare of any mission hospital in East Africa. The quality of training he helped develop at the nursing school is as good as any in Western civilization. All staff members in this health ministry must profess Jesus as Lord and Savior, and maintain high Christian standards.

Dr. and Mrs. Fraley also assisted and worked with the Kenyan government in obtaining licenses for many of the long- and short-term missionary doctors and nurses entering the country. He participated with missionaries from different missions organizations in Bible study and prayer groups. He was the attending physician for missionaries of all denominations that came into the country, and sat on the Board of Mission for Essential Drugs for 10 years, an organization he helped establish to get medicines at cost for Mission Health Services. He served as board member and vice treasurer of the Christian Health Association of Kenya for 10 years. This organization was developed to serve all of the Protestant Health Services in Kenya, consisting of some 260 units.

The president of Kenya asked the health ministries that my brother oversaw to take over a major health center in a remote area of the country among the poor. He agreed to do this, not only to meet the desperate needs of these people, but also because it would be a great opportunity to share the love and salvation of our Lord Jesus Christ. All of the 57 health units under his direction minister to the poor and needy in remote areas.

I have barely scratched the surface of all that happened over the years he spent on the mission field. God blessed them to lead a team of committed Christians to work with in developing these many ministries. Only the power and anointing of the Holy Spirit could have given a man the strength to accomplish everything he did.

My brother and his wife are among those godly servants who forsook their family ties, material possessions, home and country to follow the call of our Lord Jesus to serve the poor and needy of the world. They labored selflessly, day in and day out, to share the love of Jesus. They stood the test of time in their obedience and faithfulness.

RESTORATION AND REVIVAL

Stories illustrating Satan's use of deception can be counterbalanced by accounts of repentance, restoration and incredibly fruitful lives. This is not only God's desire for individuals, but for our once-great nation as well. My constant prayer is for another moving of God's Spirit that will touch the churches of our land, and in turn profoundly affect America for the good. As there were periodic times of revival in Old Testament Israel that saved a generation or even two, I believe this can happen in our day as well. For the sake of our children and grandchildren and countless lost souls who have yet to experience the healing touch of Jesus, I pray for a mighty spiritual reawakening that shakes our country to its core. Such a time of renewal would once again allow God's people in this land the privilege of being salt and light as our Lord and Savior preached.

The battle rages. What the outcome will be, I can't rightfully say. I only know that the enemy is not going to back off in his attacks. Like it or not, we are living in a spiritual war zone. As with my brother, who came to his senses, some of you may find this to be a jarring revelation.

QUESTIONS FOR GROUP DISCUSSION AND/OR TO BE ANSWERED INDIVIDUALLY

What aspect of the eagle story stood out the most to you? Can you give a personal example, or examples, where you have been deceived?

_____

_____

_____

_____

_____

_____

The second story, about Dr. Charles Fraley, has a better ending than the first. What made this possible?

_____

_____

_____

_____

_____

_____

One of God's great specialties is healing broken people. Why do you think some people miss out on this?

_____

_____

_____

_____

_____

_____

What makes most people uncomfortable talking about Satan? How comfortable are you when many today don't believe such a being exists?

_____

_____

_____

_____

_____

_____

A vision of the head of a beast hovering over America and swallowing, or overcoming, Christians is most alarming. In your opinion, is this a fair depiction of what is happening in our land? Why or why not?

_____

_____

_____

_____

_____

_____

Is your response to the word _revival_ positive or negative? Explain why.

_____

_____

_____

_____

_____

_____

_____

CHAPTER EIGHT

JESUS' PROPHECY
OF DECEPTION IN AMERICA

I n the days of Noah, God warned of a coming catastrophe. God
warned Lot before He destroyed wicked Sodom. I believe God has
also warned the people of America in our day. His warnings have
come through various Christian leaders who have made clear that our
nation is racing toward a day of judgment. However, one of God's most
significant warnings concerning spiritual deception in these last days
came from His Son Jesus.

Jesus warned, **"Just as it was in the days of Noah, so also will it be
in the days of the Son of Man. People were eating, drinking, marrying and being given in marriage up to the day Noah entered the ark.
Then the flood came and destroyed them all. It was the same in the
days of Lot. People were eating and drinking, buying and selling,
planting and building. But the day Lot left Sodom, fire and sulfur
rained down from heaven and destroyed them all. It will be just like
this on the day the Son of Man is revealed"** (Luke 17:26-30).

Notice that there is something missing in this passage! Jesus
doesn't mention the many evils that marked those earlier days, which
is what we usually hear about. Nor does He say anything about gross
sins in our day. In fact, not one of the items He mentions is a sin. They
are the everyday things people do in life: drink, eat, marry, buy, sell,
plant and build. It is important to recognize this in order to properly
understand the meaning of His prophecy.

The Old Testament states that in the days of Noah and Lot, lawlessness and permissiveness were rampant. It is given as a basic reason God destroyed both places. Yet when comparing our day to those, Jesus doesn't make a single comment about this. His comparison is with the buying, selling, eating, drinking, marrying, planting and building. He only mentions these everyday affairs of life! WHY?

The answer takes us to the core of the spiritual deception now taking place in our country. It helps explain why our society's moral values have deteriorated so quickly. Everyone knows about the sins of our land; we hear about them every day. Jesus did not have to mention them. David Wilkerson, Pastor of Times Square Church in New York City stated, *"I was listening to a special radio program in a large eastern city, where the people on the street were being interviewed about the moral condition of America. The question was asked, 'Do you believe America has lost its moral integrity?' Almost all who were interviewed said basically the same thing. 'America is going to hell in a hand basket!' 'We no longer care if scoundrels run our country, as long as we prosper.' 'Anything goes now; we are in the last days of our society—we are modern Rome going into collapse!' 'Morality and purity have been sold out to pleasure and prosperity.' 'Sodom had no porno, no Internet sex, no abortion, no filthy television polluting that society, so how can America expect to go on without being held accountable?'"*

In this warning from God's Son that compares our day to the days of Noah and Lot, I see the Lord pouring out His love to the majority of the people rather than chastising the minority who are involved in wickedness. <u>We are the Lord's main concern in this warning</u>. We are those who go about doing the things most people do in the normal way of living—the buying, selling, building, marrying, and so forth.

Why are we Jesus' main concern in His warning, rather than those who are involved in gross sins? I believe it is because He could foresee our <u>over-commitment</u> to everyday affairs. What we are doing is not a sin in and of itself. The problem is the commitment of our hearts to these self-serving matters over and above a commitment to live by godly standards. Our over-extended routines have become more important to us than seeking to understand and obey God's will.

This is what happened to my brother, taking him out of God's will for his life. You and I are the ones who can help prevent our society falling apart at the seams. We are the people who can make a difference. But Jesus knew that most Christians in our day would become so wrapped up in their everyday lives that we would ignore the warning signs.

PEOPLE NOW ARE DOING LITTLE TO PREPARE THEMSELVES.

Our country is on the brink of a great chastening from the hand of God. America has been blessed far beyond most nations throughout history. The Bible says God will hold us accountable for the deterioration of our moral standards. Luke 12:48b reads, **"From everyone who has been given much, much will be demanded; and from the one who has been entrusted with much, much more will be asked."** The Scriptures teach that God disciplines those He has blessed if they become careless in their way of living. It is His way of correcting those He loves. **"My son, do not make light of the Lord's discipline, and do not lose heart when he rebukes you, because the Lord disciplines those he loves, and he punishes everyone he accepts as a son. Endure hardship as discipline; God is treating you as sons. For what son is not disciplined by his father?"** (Hebrews 12:6-7).

Just as in Noah's day, people now are doing little to prepare themselves—to build their spiritual arks. What Jesus warned us about was a deception that produces self-centered, self-serving Christians. This condition caused the Lord more concern than the many sins the minority were involved in. He was more troubled about the heart attitude of the majority. The focus of the heart was a problem in Noah's day, and it is a problem in our day as well. That is why Jesus lists the things that are everyday time-killers, even though not one of them is a sin as such.

We have become so preoccupied that our hearts have grown cold. The worldly media has deceived us and weakened our ability to discern right from wrong regarding our commitments.

Our preoccupation with these basic elements has caused us to lose our discernment in regard to interpreting the signs of the times. Jesus warned that even Christians would be deceived. **"For false Christs and false prophets will appear and perform signs and miracles to deceive the elect—if that were possible. So be on guard; I have told you everything ahead of time"** (Mark 13:22-23; see also Matthew 24:24).

> HIS FIERCEST ATTACKS
> ARE GOING TO BE
> IN THE AREA WHERE
> GOD'S PEOPLE ARE
> THE STRONGEST.

Permissiveness and lawlessness had deteriorated to the point of being out of control in the days of Noah and Lot. But Jesus says there was a greater concern—the heart attitude of the people who put their priorities above God's. This caused them to not pay attention to His desires. What they were doing was not sinful in the traditional sense of the word, but the commitment of their hearts was to self-serving rather than to walking according to the standards of God and His will for their lives. This, tragically, prevented them from seeing the signs of the times.

The truth of this prophecy is tough to discuss as I do not want to discount God's blessings. However, the spirit of the good life has created a commitment to our everyday affairs over and above our commitment to seek His will and it has captured the hearts of all too many Americans. As my brother shared in his testimony, the Lord gave him a vision of a beast over our country, overcoming Christians almost at will, through the deceptive elements of materialism and pleasure.

God chose to put these words from Jesus about Noah's day in the Bible to warn us about our day. It was important to Him that we be wise to the kind of warfare the enemy would throw at Christians in these end-times. Too many of God's people have fallen for this deception and become victims of his attacks. The Scriptures certainly caution us about these matters—we have just failed to heed the warnings.

PRELUDE TO IDENTIFYING SATAN'S PLAN OF SPIRITUAL WARFARE

The nation of Israel had a special calling from God. In the days before the Lord's First Coming, the enemy had deceived the people to where most of them had completely fallen away from their unique calling. This happened in the very country where God's presence had been greatest. That is how the enemy works! His fiercest attacks are going to be in the area where God's people are the strongest, especially if they have a special calling from God.

Is the Body of Christ in America repeating history? The fruit of our nation in this last generation reveals that we too are falling away from our calling in these days prior to the Second Coming. As with Israel, it is happening in the part of the world where God's presence has been the strongest.

SPIRITUAL ATTACK

My study on this topic began in the spring of 1971. At that time, after my wife and I were obedient to the leading of the Lord to take in six additional children, He began to open my eyes to the tremendous spiritual warfare the enemy was waging against biblical values in America. Now, almost four decades later, these truths are even more evident than they were back then. Please remember these facts:

One: The spiritual development of America reveals that we have a special calling from God. Other than the nation of Israel, there has never been another country in which God has intervened to the degree He has in the spiritual development of America.

Two: In any endeavor, when things are deteriorating as our fruit reveals, it is always wise to review fundamentals. This principle is true in business, sports, personal relationships, etc., and it is true in our commitment to the basics of Christianity.

Three: It is important to develop an understanding of what is causing the problem. As we saw in the past few chapters, the history of God's people reveals that Satan has always used either persecution or deception against them. The Bible warns us about his tactics. The way he will deploy his methods will primarily be through the kingdom of the world, or society, and its systems.

Four: Satan is <u>executing</u> his deception against the fundamentals of Christianity in America, and his plan has been incredibly successful in this last generation. <u>Identifying how he is working is key to any corrective action</u>. This is what will free us from the spiritual chains that are binding so many American Christians to the standards of the world's kingdom.

SPIRITUAL WARFARE, NOT PHYSICAL

The warfare in which we are engaged is not a physical one. Our battle is not against flesh and blood but against the spiritual forces of evil (see Ephesians 6:10-13). My interest is not just the saving of America as a physical entity in the kingdom of the world, but more about <u>saving the mission of Christianity in America</u>. I am a patriotic person; I love our country and am grateful for the freedom our forefathers secured. However, I fear that what we have enjoyed will not last long once the enemy has deceived the Body of Christ into straying from the path of righteousness.

AMERICA IN BIBLE PROPHECY

Have you ever wondered why America, the greatest superpower in history and a center of Christianity, is not mentioned in Bible prophecy? The results of my research revealed that America actually does play a major role in the last days. Because my approach is new and somewhat overwhelming, I had some of my interpretation of end-times prophetic Scriptures reviewed by Greek-language scholars. Not one disagreed with what I found, or saw it as unfounded. When you read these words as to what the Greek means, do not reject them until you compare what I say to what the Bible says. These comments are especially important regarding what I will share about Revelation 13. I will give you a meaning for every descriptive word or phrase as it relates to America.

<u>Revelation Chapter 13 is key to understanding spiritual warfare in these last days.</u> My brother's vision of a "beast" hovering over America and deceiving Christians, knowing America is a great center of Christianity and knowing Satan has always viciously attacked anything that God raises up, I did diligent research to see if America fit into this end-times prophecy. Revelation 13 involves what in prophetic language is called a "beast." These thoughts plus knowing the moral values in our country were deteriorating so rapidly, added to the devotion I gave to closely examining this spiritual warfare chapter.

No one can be harmed by investigation. Whether it leads to truth or falsehood, the investigator reaps a reward for undertaking the search. If it leads to truth, the investigator would have missed it if he had not made the effort. If it leads to falsehood, the investigator has still been strengthened from the experience. Knowing what we believe and why, always gives us a more sound and sure faith.

> MY RESEARCH REVEALED THAT AMERICA PLAYS A MAJOR ROLE IN THE LAST DAYS.

If my research seems somewhat overwhelming, this is not an unusual response to Bible prophecy. It has been the experience of God's people throughout history concerning prophetic Scriptures. Recall the Israelites and their refusal to accept Jesus as Messiah, even though He fulfilled more than 500 Bible prophecies! Unfortunately, their minds were closed! They were looking for a powerful earthly king and kingdom from which they would profit. The message of Jesus was about a spiritual kingdom, so the majority rejected Jesus and His message.

INTRODUCTION TO SATAN'S END-TIMES BATTLE PLAN

An obvious theme of the book of Revelation is the ongoing battle between good and evil. Behind the beast in chapter 13 is the dragon, or Satan, whose purpose has always been to frustrate the rule of God. Before summarizing Revelation 13, I need to review some important truths in Revelation 12 as it is a lead-in to 13. In chapter 12 John paints a word picture of the warfare that has been going on since the earliest times. Chapter 12 describes that ongoing conflict symbolically. In it is an overview of some of the major events in God's plan for both the salvation of mankind and to protect Israel after the birth of the Savior.

Revelation's 12th chapter opens with a great sign in the sky. **"A great and wondrous sign appeared in the heaven; a woman clothed with the sun, with the moon under her feet and a crown of twelve stars on her head"** (12:1). I understand this woman to be the nation of Israel. The twelve stars are the twelve tribes. The sun and moon are elements of God's creation that help control various functions on earth.

"She was pregnant and cried out in pain as she was about to give birth" (Revelation 12:2). This verse speaks of the purpose God intended for Israel from the time of Abraham, which was to give birth to His Son (see Galatians 3:16-29), the Christ or the Messiah. The Old Testament chronicles these birth pains, which lasted 2000 years.

"Then another sign appeared in heaven: an enormous red dragon with seven heads and ten horns and seven crowns on his heads" (Revelation 12:3). Verse 9 tells us that the dragon is Satan. The full meaning of the symbolic language of "seven heads and ten horns and seven crowns on his heads" is explained in my discussion of chapter 13; it speaks of an earthly power or authority. Coupling Satan with this earthly power is expected, as the devil's kingdom is of this world. In this verse The Roman Empire is this earthly power.

"His tail swept a third of the stars out of the sky and flung them to the earth. The dragon stood in front of the woman who was about to give birth, so that he might devour her child the moment

it was born" (Revelation 12:4). God put this picture in John's prophecy to show the power of Satan's forces. The second part of the verse informs us that Satan knew Jesus would be born, and stood ready to kill Him at the first opportunity. We are told in the Bible that such an attempt was made when Satan motivated King Herod to give orders to kill all the boys in Bethlehem two years old and younger. This was foretold by the prophet Jeremiah (see Jeremiah 31:18), and we are told in Matthew 2:18 that this event fulfilled his prophecy.

"She [the woman/Israel] **gave birth to a son, a male child, who will rule all the nations with an iron scepter. And her child was snatched** ["caught" is a more accurate translation of the Greek] **up to God and his throne"** (Revelation 12:5). Of course, Jesus was the male child to whom Israel gave birth. He returned to Heaven after living on Earth for about 33 1/2 years. Notice that John doesn't just say Jesus returned to Heaven, but to the <u>throne</u> of God, which indicates His deity.

"The woman [people of Israel] **fled into the desert to a place prepared for her by God, where she might be taken care of for 1260 days"** (Revelation 12:6). A major historical event happened to the people of Israel within the generation after the Ascension of Jesus. The Romans dispersed them throughout the world, but they were protected by God and have kept their identity as a race for 2000 years. Now centuries later, the race that descended from Abraham has been re-established in their homeland, Palestine. 1260 days is explained later.

"And there was war in heaven, Michael and his angels fought against the dragon, and the dragon and his angels fought back. But he was not strong enough, and they lost their place in heaven. The great dragon was hurled down—that ancient serpent called the devil or Satan, who leads the whole world astray. He was hurled to the earth, and his angels with him" (Revelation 12:7-9). After the Resurrection of Jesus there was a war in Heaven between the forces of the archangel Michael and Satan and his legions. Satan and his angels were defeated. They lost their place in Heaven and were hurled to the Earth. I certainly do not understand all that takes place in the spiritual realm beyond what Scripture tells me. I know that in the beginning, Satan was present in the Garden of Eden, and he has been active on Earth throughout history. However, after this war and losing his place in Heaven, history confirms his activity on earth has increased.

"Then I heard a loud voice in heaven say: 'Now have come the salvation and the power and the kingdom of our God, and the authority of his Christ. For the accuser of our brothers, who accuses them before our God day and night, has been hurled down. They overcame him by the blood of the Lamb and by the word of their testimony; they did not love their lives so much as to shrink from death'" (Revelation 12:10-11).

> JOHN MAKES AN IMPORTANT FACT KNOWN IN REVELATION 12:12 THAT WE SELDOM HEAR DISCUSSED.

The word <u>now</u> in this verse is key because it tells us when these things of God took place. Ephesians 1:18-21 reveals exactly when that time was. **"I pray also that the eyes of your heart may be enlightened in order that you may know the hope to which he has called you, the riches of his glorious inheritance in the saints, and his incomparable great power for us who believe. That power is like the working of his mighty strength, which he exerted in Christ when he raised him from the dead and seated him at his right hand** [at His throne, as stated earlier in Revelation 12:5] **in the heavenly realms, far above all rule and authority, power and dominion, and every title that can be given, not only in the present age but also in the one to come"** (Ephesians 1:18-21). The salvation of mankind came through the blood of the Lamb on the cross. The power of the Kingdom of God and the authority of Christ came when God raised Jesus from the grave and seated Him at His right hand. It was when Jesus was crucified and rose from the dead that victory was won, and Satan and his angels were hurled down to Earth, and the power and authority of Jesus came into being.

Because of the salvation, power and authority of Jesus, John makes another important fact known in Revelation 12:12 that <u>we seldom hear discussed</u>. **"Therefore rejoice you heavens and you who dwell in them! But woe to the earth and the sea, because the devil has gone down to you! He is filled with fury, because he knows that his time is short."** <u>This is one of the most powerful warnings to the people of God found in Scripture</u>. **"Woe to the earth and the sea, because the devil has gone down to you! He is filled with fury, because he knows that his time is short."** Much of the balance of Revelation 12 describes the protection afforded the woman (Israel) following the birth of the male child (Jesus) after Satan and his angels had been hurled to Earth.

"When the dragon saw that he had been hurled to the earth, he pursued the woman who had given birth to the male child. The woman was given the two wings of a great eagle, so that she might fly to the place prepared for her in the desert, where she would be taken care of for a time, times and half a time, out of the serpent's [Satan's] **reach"** (Revelation 12:13-14). In my research I discovered that the phrase "time, times and half a time" was used by Jewish scribes to refer to an unknown troublesome period of time that lingers—and lingers—and lingers.

Recall verse 6: **"The woman fled into the desert to a place prepared for her by God, where she might be taken care of for 1,260 days."** 1260 days refers to the same unknown period of time that God would protect the nation of Israel from Satan. The phrase "time, times and half a time" is taken from Daniel 7:25. It, or something similar, appears as well in Daniel 12:7, Revelation 11:2-3, 12:6 and 13:5. According to Jewish history, when John wrote this book, they had no way by their calendar to express an extended period of time.

The Jewish calendar consisted of 12 equal months, each with 30 days corresponding to the approximate cycle of the moon. Therefore, 1260 days would be one year, two years and one half of a year. To align the length of their year with the solar year, a complete cycle of the Earth around the sun, every 2 or 3 years they would add an extension. We do something similar with our leap year every 4th year.

Of course we know the dispersion of the Jewish people lasted for more than 1800 years, but as John prophesied God protected them and their national identity. One of the things I found in my research is that in prophecy, numbers are often used symbolically. Therefore, the meaning of the number rather than the actual count of the number, is what is important.

The next two verses finish what John began in verses 13-14 about God protecting His people Israel. **"Then from his mouth the serpent spewed water like a river, to overtake the woman and sweep her away with the torrent. But the earth helped the woman by opening its mouth and swallowing the river that the dragon had spewed out of his mouth"** (Revelation 12:15-16). In A.D. 70, the Roman army destroyed Jerusalem, which began the period of "time, times and half a time." We now can see that it refers to the Diaspora of over 1800 years. Many Jews fled to Italy and Spain, and some as far away as China. Scattered elements settled throughout Europe; however, Spain was the center of Jewish life until 1492. During the Spanish Inquisition, they were expelled after a century of persecution by the then-ruling Catholic Church. From there they settled in Europe in countries like Germany, Poland and even Russia. Usually they lived in city districts or remote territories, which were occupied only by Jewish people. This continued until the Nazi massacres of the 1930s and 1940s, when as many as two-fifths of the world's Jewish people lost their lives.

The persecution of the Jews provoked many to begin to search for a way to return to their homeland. This culminated with the creation of the State of Israel when the United Nations recognized their new nation on May 14, 1948. Through the many years of dispersion and persecution, God fulfilled His promise to Abraham and preserved his descendants. This second restoration to Palestine, reviewed in chapter 2, was prophesied in Isaiah 11:11-12, Jeremiah 16:14-15 and Ezekiel 11:16-17. Since May 14, 1948 the Jewish people have continued to battle for their homeland. In fact, the small land of Palestine and the nation that occupies it is often front-page news today.

Beginning with the next verse, we see the picture changes. The Jewish people being preserved by God, Satan went off to make war against her offspring, who are Christians.

"Then the dragon was enraged at the woman and went off to make war against the rest of her offspring—those who obey God's commandments <u>and hold to the testimony of Jesus</u>" (Revelation 12:17). For nearly 2000 years, Satan has attacked Christians through relentless persecution and deception. As we already noted, nearly 70 million Christians have been killed since the church began. More than 43 million of these were killed in the last 100 years. Of course many more have been imprisoned or persecuted in other ways. Spiritual warfare is for real. It is not a game!

The pronouncement **"woe to the earth and the sea, because the devil has gone down to you! He is filled with fury, because he knows that his time is short"** and "[the dragon] **went off to make war against the rest of her offspring—those who obey God's commandments and hold to the testimony of Jesus"** has certainly been true regarding the church.

Like His words about the days of Noah and Lot, this too is a word to us from Jesus. Remember that all of the Book of Revelation is a message Jesus Christ gave to John about what was to come to pass. **"The message of Jesus Christ, which God gave him to show His servants what must soon take place. He made it known by sending His angel to His servant John who testifies to everything he saw—that is the word of God and the testimony of Jesus Christ"** (Revelation 1:1-2).

Having finished chapter 12, we are now ready to turn to Revelation 13 and the prophecy about the "beast" that will rise to power during the last days.

QUESTIONS FOR GROUP DISCUSSION AND/OR
TO BE ANSWERED INDIVIDUALLY

What kind of "everyday affairs of life" would you say have made American Christians less sensitive to more important spiritual priorities?

_____

_____

_____

_____

_____

_____

In what ways do you see the church in these days prior to our Lord's return acting like Israel prior to Jesus' First Coming?

_____

_____

_____

_____

_____

_____

Give your understanding of Ephesians 6:12, which states that our battle is not against flesh and blood but against the spiritual forces of evil.

_____

_____

_____

_____

_____

_____

In the past 100 years, more than 43 **million** Christians have been martyred. How aware of this have you been? In what way(s) is this significant to you personally?

_____

_____

_____

_____

_____

_____

Do you believe America has a major place in Bible prophecy? If so, what modifications in your life should you make?

_____

_____

_____

_____

_____

_____

Are there further questions you have about Revelation chapter 12?

_____

_____

_____

_____

_____

_____

CHAPTER NINE

THE BEAST OF REVELATION 13

After Satan was hurled to Earth, we were warned that he would furiously war against Christians. The history of the church over the last 2000 years confirms this to be the case.

America was founded on Christian values, and because God often intervened in our nation's spiritual development, we eventually became the world's center of Christianity. Satan has always schemed to destroy anything God raises up. In this last generation, two unique things happened in our history: first, we became the greatest superpower in the history of mankind; and second, even though there are now hundreds of thousands of churches in America, thousands of evangelistic outreach ministries and the Bible taught everyday throughout our nation on radio and TV, our moral values have deteriorated more in this last generation than in all of the years combined since the beginning of our country.

Knowing these things, we should at least consider the possibility of America fitting into the Revelation 13 "spiritual warfare" prophecy about the last days. Could our nation be the "beast" or superpower that this chapter says eventually overcomes the testimony of Christians in the last days?

There is a sure way to find out. It is to put this possibility to a sound scriptural test.

Before I do that, I want to lay out some basic guidelines for use when interpreting prophetic Scriptures.

1. **There is no higher authority for understanding God's Word than to refer to other Scriptures where a similar word or phrase is used. This is what Jesus often did.** This is the most important guideline, because we are going to the source of that inspiration rather than simply using speculation and conjecture to try to interpret. If an interpretation holds for one passage, it should for another as well. What's more, the Word of God is absolutely accurate. We may not always understand everything it says, but we should not try to come up with an idea unless it can be documented accurately with Scripture.

2. **In order to understand a word or passage, it is often necessary to study the original language in which it was written.** The Old Testament was written mostly in Hebrew, and the New Testament in Greek. Difficult passages often require learning what that word or phrase meant to the Hebrew or Greek author who wrote it. This is especially true with prophetic words and phrases.

3. **Historical evidence either confirms that a prophecy has already been fulfilled or is yet to be.** Prophesies are statements about future events. Either they have happened as foretold, or they haven't. The evidence should be conclusive.

4. **Words in prophecy sometimes are used differently than their literal meaning.** A word in prophecy may have a symbolic meaning rather than a concrete one. This will become evident as we proceed.

The Revelation 13 depiction of the "beast" is one of the most detailed and exacting descriptions of anything in the Bible. Evidently God did not want any mistake being made as to its identity. There are many theories today on the identity of this "beast," in Revelation 13, but I couldn't find any that can say they have run a scriptural test on each word and phrase to confirm their view.

IDENTIFYING THE BEAST OF REVELATION 13

John prophesies, **"And the dragon** [Satan] **stood on the shore of the** sea. **And I saw a beast coming out of the sea. He had ten horns and seven heads, with ten crowns on his horns, and on each head a blasphemous name"** (Revelation 13:1). Although these words seem difficult, if not impossible to decipher, they are actually a blessing from the Lord to keep us from being misled. A careful reading of this verse reveals six distinct elements we need to test to determine the identity of this "beast" or superpower. If I can demonstrate that since World War II, America began fulfilling all of John's prophecies about this "beast" in Revelation 13, then the enemy has come up with a most deceptive method to keep Christians in America from fulfilling our mission to be the **salt of the earth** and the **light of the world** in these last days.

The six descriptive words and phrases in this verse are: **(1) "beast"; (2) "coming out of the sea"; (3) "ten horns"; (4) "seven heads"; (5) "ten crowns on his horns";** and **(6) "on each head a blasphemous name."**

Test #1: the "beast." The actual meaning of "beast" as used in prophecy should be abundantly clear. Remember that God's inspired Word is the highest authority anyone can use to determine the meaning of a word in Scripture.

Fortunately, the Old Testament prophet Daniel speaks of "beasts" in chapter seven, and he is actually told the meaning by an angel. I suggest reading all of Daniel 7, but here are some highlights that help determine the meaning of this word "beast" in prophecy.

"In the first year of Belshazzar king of Babylon, Daniel had a dream, and visions passed through his mind as he was lying on his bed. He wrote down the substance of his dream. Daniel said: 'In my vision at night I looked, and there before me were the four winds of heaven churning up the great sea. Four great beasts, each different from the others, came up out of the sea'" (Daniel 7:1-3). **"I, Daniel, was troubled in spirit, and the visions that passed through my mind disturbed me. I approached one of those standing there and asked him the true meaning of all this. So he told me and gave me the interpretation of these things: The four great beasts are four kingdoms that will rise from the earth"** (Daniel 7:15-17).

According to the interpretation given to Daniel, the word "beast" in prophetic Scripture refers to a kingdom, an empire, or <u>what we would call a superpower</u>. Elsewhere in the Book of Daniel, the four "beasts" he saw are described as the superpowers of Babylon, Media-Persia, Greece (under Alexander the Great) and the Roman Empire. In the first part of chapter seven Daniel also describes three of the "beasts" as wild animals—a lion, bear and leopard. Note that John uses all three of these animals in Revelation 13:2 to describe the "beast" he saw, indicating that the Revelation 13 "beast" is the greatest superpower in the history of mankind. This is what America has become in this last generation.

> "COMING OUT OF THE SEA" INVOLVES A CULTURALLY AND ETHNICALLY DIVERSE NATION.

Daniel used the word "beast" to describe the recognized world powers, and John uses this word in the same way when writing about a superpower that will rise up in the era of those who give testimony to Jesus Christ in the last days. America passes the test of being a "beast," in a prophetic sense, because we have become that world superpower.

Let me pause briefly to explain something. The "beast" in Revelation 13 is often said to refer to a man. Some Bible translations actually refer to this "beast" as a man; other versions call it an entity or superpower. For example, the King James and New International Versions use the masculine pronouns <u>"he," "his" and "him,"</u> when referring to the "beast," which suggests the "beast" is a man. The Revised Standard Version, Philips and others use the neuter pronoun <u>"it," and "its"</u> when referring to the "beast," which indicates the "beast" is a superpower, not a person.

To properly interpret the word, I contacted a seminary professor with a doctorate in Greek. Were the pronouns <u>"he," "his," and "him"</u> correct, or were <u>"it" and "its"</u> correct?

The <u>noun</u> translated "beast" in Revelation 13 is the Greek word *onpiov*.

The Greek word *avrov* is the <u>pronoun</u> Revelation 13 uses to reference the "beast." To be grammatically correct, a <u>pronoun</u> must be of the <u>same gender as the noun</u> it refers to. If the original Greek word used for "beast" is <u>masculine gender</u>, then <u>"he," "his" and "him"</u> are the correct pronouns; if the original Greek word is <u>neuter gender</u>, then <u>"it" and "its"</u> are the proper translation.

The Greek word for "beast" in Revelation 13 is <u>neuter</u> gender, so <u>"it" and "its"</u> are the correct pronouns. This is a grammatical fact. Most publishers agree that to use the masculine gender pronouns <u>"he," "his," and "him"</u> when referring to the word "beast" is an inaccurate translation (see Zondervan Publishing House, *Greek-English New Testament*, Grand Rapids, MI, 1975, p. 751). Let me repeat: The Greek word for "beast" is <u>neuter</u> gender, so the proper rendering of John's writing is the pronouns <u>"it" and "its."</u> Thus, like Daniel, John likely used the word "beast" to refer to a superpower, not an individual.

Interpreting John's use of the prophetic word "beast" to mean a superpower is also consistent with the first guideline, which is to use other Scriptures—in this case, the Book of Daniel. Granted, superpowers have leaders, even as Babylon did in Daniel's day. But it would be an error to see this passage as first referring to a person instead of a superpower.

Test #2: "coming out of the sea." This phrase also appears in Daniel. So the angel's interpretation of Daniel's vision can also be used to understand John's vision. Daniel writes, **"Four great beasts, each different from the others, came up out of the sea"** (7:3). Daniel's four beasts (Daniel 7:1-7) refer to a succession of world powers that shaped Israel's history before the time of Christ. The lion represents Babylon, which conquered Egypt in 606 B.C. and achieved political prominence in the Middle East. The bear is the Media-Persian Empire. They conquered the Babylonians in about 539 B.C. and ruled until 331 B.C., when Alexander the Great defeated them (Daniel 8:21). The leopard represents the Greek Empire under Alexander, which splintered into four separate kingdoms as Daniel prophesied it would (Daniel 8:8, 8:22). The last of these four kingdoms continued until 31 B.C., when, as Daniel prophesied (8:9-12, 23-25), the Roman Empire rose to power.

In Daniel's account, a succession of peoples from different geographic bases conquered one another, bringing together people from Africa, Asia and Europe in a mixture of customs, cultures and languages. From this historical review, we can infer that **"coming out of the sea"** involves a culturally and ethnically diverse empire or nation. This fits with Revelation 17:15, which reads, **"'The waters you saw ... are peoples, multitudes, nations and languages.'"** As a nation of immigrants, the United States fits this description. Europeans and Africans joined indigenous peoples of North America during the Colonial Period, followed by waves of immigrants from all parts of the Earth in the 19th and 20th centuries. Together, these people make up America, which is often called a "nation of nations."

The peopling of America is one of the great dramas in history. Over the years a stream of humanity crossed continents and oceans to reach the United States. They came speaking many languages and representing almost every nationality, race and religion. Today, there are more people of Irish ancestry in the United States than in Ireland, more Jews than in Israel, and more blacks than in most African countries. There are more Polish people in Detroit alone than in most of Poland's major cities, and more than twice as many people of Italian descent in New York as there are in Venice.

The setting in which the history of these people has unfolded is as impressive as the diversity of the peoples themselves. The United States is the largest cultural-linguistic unit in the world. The distance from San Francisco to Boston is the same as from Madrid to Moscow. Yet, we have one primary language, one set of federal laws and one economy. This same area in Europe is fragmented into numerous nations, languages and competing military and political blocs.

The "melting pot" was once a popular image of American assimilation. The largest single ethnic strain is of European ancestry, the region of the old Roman Empire. Daniel prophesied in chapter 7 that another power, a new country, would rise up out of the people of the old Roman Empire. It would become stronger than any of the other powers. He even states that this new power will defeat three of the powers out of the old Roman Empire, which we did: England, France and Spain.

Daniel prophesied about superpowers that affected the history of Israel. Therefore he would not have prophesied of any superpower after the Roman Empire, until Israel once again became a nation, which was soon after World War II when we gained superpower status. America fits the descriptive characteristic of the "beast" **"coming out of the sea."**

Test #3: "ten horns." Understanding the biblical use of the phrase *"ten horns"* requires an interpretation of both words.

Many numbers in Scripture have a symbolic meaning beyond their actual numerical value. Bible scholars have written entire books on these meanings. Such studies have deduced that *"ten"* stands for all-encompassing. Examples of ten in Scripture include the Ten Commandments and the ten plagues. In these examples, ten is used to mean an exact count. Numbers in prophecy, however, are often symbolic. For example, in Revelation 12:3, John uses the phrase *"ten horns"* when describing The Roman Empire used by the red dragon, Satan, even though Rome ruled about 27 other nations. Daniel also used the number *"ten"* in chapter 7 in a symbolic way to indicate might that is all-encompassing.

The second word in this descriptive phrase is *"horns."* Throughout the Bible, *"horns"* are a common symbol of strength. In the Book of Daniel, the word represents nations. Presumably, John too is using *"horns"* to mean nations. These would be nations with substantial power and influence but less than that of a "beast" or superpower. The beast in Revelation 13 has *"ten horns,"* so this suggests that the superpower has great influence over other powerful nations.

The United States is a nation of superpower status. Of course there are other powerful nations (horns) in the world today. Japan and

Germany are economic powers; Russia is still a military power. France and England are former colonial powers that still wield political influence. But only the United States can claim to be a superpower. We exercise a certain amount of economic, military, political, influence over many of the world's lesser powers.

Another interpretation of *"ten horns"* says they represent the nations allied in the European Union. But the EU does not meet all of the other descriptive phrases in Revelation 13 that describe this end-time superpower. To be valid, an interpretation must fit every word and phrase the Lord has given us to identify this superpower of the last days. That is why each of these descriptions is included—so we don't have to guess. America passes the test of having *"ten horns."*

Test #4: "seven heads." The explanation of *"seven heads"* is fairly simple. Seven throughout Scripture denotes completeness. God completed creation in *seven* days. Joshua was commanded to march around the city of Jericho for *seven* days. On the *seventh* day, the priests and the army marched around the city *seven* times. When this was completed, the walls fell. Elisha told the military captain Naaman to dip himself seven times in the Jordan River and he would be healed. Like the number *ten*, *seven* is symbolic when used in prophetic phrases.

The word *heads* simply means *leadership*. For John to prophesy that this "beast" or superpower would have *seven heads* states that its leadership would be complete in all areas of world affairs. It would dominate—be number one—in commerce, industrial output, production of goods and services, agriculture, military might, political power, economic wealth, and so on.

"Seven heads" means that this end-times superpower would enjoy superiority, or be complete, in all areas of international influence. Since World War II we have developed the position in world affairs that would allow John to make this prophecy about us.

Test #5: "ten crowns on his horns." Of all the characteristics of the "beast" or superpower in Revelation 13, **"ten crowns on his horns"** is truly unique. It is a demanding characteristic. The word *"crown"* (or *"diadem"* as some versions read) was a distinctive mark of royalty among the early Greeks and Romans. If the word *crown* or *diadem* is used, something is being said about its political position.

To use the word *crowns* with *horns* indicates this prophetic phrase <u>is describing the political position of these *horns* or nations</u> that the super-power in Revelation 13 influences. Allow me to break down this phrase. *Ten* means all-encompassing, *crowns* means political position, and *horns* references various powerful countries. When John writes that the crowns (political control) were positioned on the horns (each nation), he means that each country has its own governing political body. So this superpower in the last days allows those nations under its influence to retain political autonomy.

> THE SUPERPOWER ALLOWS THOSE NATIONS UNDER ITS INFLUENCE TO RETAIN POLITICAL AUTONOMY.

If the superpower described in Revelation 13:1 politically controlled these other countries, then Scripture would have said *ten crowns on his head* to reflect the beast's political leadership over these countries. It would <u>not</u> have placed the *crowns on the horns*.

The U.S. is the only superpower I know of that has met this distinctive characteristic. For example, we helped defeat both Japan and Germany in World War II, yet we allowed each country to retain political autonomy. In fact, we helped rebuild the countries we conquered.

This imagery of crowns and horns, of politics and nations, is a telling description of our relationship with other nations. America's influence reaches across the globe. Missionaries have journeyed to the remotest parts of the Earth and found American brand names, TV shows and popular music. The United States maintains more military bases and foreign embassies than any other nation, and its technological, industrial and commercial influence draw even more of the world's population into its grasp. Yet none of these people owe allegiance to the American flag. Few of those under American influence are actually U.S. citizens.

How aptly John's phrase of crowns and horns describes America's influence: These nations are heavily influenced by our culture and commerce, but not ruled by our laws. We pass this unique test God gives to describe this end-time superpower.

Test number six: "on each head a blasphemous name." We need to examine the word *blasphemy*. Without a proper understanding of this sin, it would be difficult to comprehend how it relates to the heads of the beasts or to aspects of their leadership.

THE LEADERSHIP MISUSES THE SACRED NAME OF GOD.

Throughout the Old Testament, blasphemy was one of the gravest sins one could commit. To blaspheme is to make light or sport of the name and sovereignty of God. In the New Testament, the Greek word for *blasphemy* means to injure one's reputation. The Scriptures are strict in teaching that the holy name of God is sacred. To misuse His name in any way that is not marked with a sense of awe and majesty is viewed as blasphemy.

To better understand blasphemy, think about what happened prior to the Crucifixion. Jesus was true deity, but the Sanhedrin did not accept Him as such, and the high priest condemned Him to death for what this religious leader deemed blasphemy. The seriousness of this sin is shown by the fact that it was punishable by death. So when Jesus acknowledged His deity, the religious leaders claimed he had misused the name of God, or blasphemed.

In describing the superpower in Revelation 13, when John speaks of the blasphemous name on each head, it means the leadership of our government will misuse the sacred name of God after becoming the world superpower. John indicates that in each area of leadership—each head—this last-days superpower will use the sacred name of God irreverently in carrying out unrighteous acts. This would mean our government promotes a worldly cause while claiming an association with the name of God. This is, in fact, what has begun to happen in this last generation as our government started to pass laws that promote sin. Examples include promoting sexual promiscuity in schools by passing out condoms, sponsoring the murder of millions of unborn babies through abortion, and outlawing praying aloud in school.

Undoubtedly, many of our nation's founders submitted to the Lord's direction. But on our way to worldwide superiority in this last generation, we have abandoned our forefathers' godly principles. Other governments engage in wicked activities. But no other nation claims God's blessing while it commits such evil. We easily pass the sixth test of Revelation 13:1 that the Lord gave us to identify this superpower in the last days.

If this verse had been written in contemporary English, and the symbols were replaced with their contemporary explanations, it might read something like this:

And I saw a world superpower develop in a new country made up of people from many nationalities. It influenced other powerful nations throughout the world; it held a position of leadership in every area of world affairs, although it did not try to politically rule other countries—they were allowed to govern themselves. It used the name of God freely and irreverently in many of its worldly activities.

The following is a quick reference to the words and phrases in verse one that characterizes the superpower in Revelation 13.

BEAST: Empire or superpower.

OUT OF THE SEA: A nation of peoples from diverse cultural and ethnic backgrounds.

NUMERAL TEN: All-encompassing.

HORNS: Nations with significant power, authority and influence, but not superpowers.

NUMERAL SEVEN: Completeness.

HEADS: Leadership.

CROWNS OR DIADEM: A distinct mark of royalty or political position.

BLASPHEMY: To supposedly diminish God by misusing His holy name.

In these last days the beast that Satan will give his complete authority to will no doubt be the greatest superpower in the history of the world. This makes a lot more sense than the devil forming an alliance with a second- or third-rate power.

America presently not only holds that position of supremacy, but also fits all of John's descriptive characteristics he gives to identify this "beast." Therefore, I would conclude that America fits into the prophecy Jesus gave to John in Revelation.

I fear Satan's ability to deceive is greater than most of us acknowledge. He is far better at pulling off the unexpected than most of us think. Because of our personal experiences with spiritual failure, we may comprehend this as individuals. Anyone who has been in a position of church leadership can also understand how all too often this scenario plays itself out in congregational settings. But few realize how true his evil ambitions are regarding nations. For American Christians to fail to heed what is being revealed here would be an error of great magnitude. Nothing would please the enemy more than to continue to deceive Christians, and increase his control of the great assets of the United States of America for his own evil purposes.

QUESTIONS FOR GROUP DISCUSSION AND/OR TO BE ANSWERED INDIVIDUALLY

Prior to reading this book, what were your thoughts about how America might fit into Bible prophecy?

_____

_____

_____

_____

_____

_____

Which of the following words most closely reflects your response to the idea of America being the beast in Revelation 13:

UNQUESTIONABLE   PROBABLE   POSSIBLE   IMPOSSIBLE

Explain why you chose the word you did.

_____

_____

_____

_____

_____

_____

_____

_____

_____

_____

_____

Of the six descriptive phrases in Revelation 13:1, which one in your mind points most convincingly to America? Why?

_____

_____

_____

_____

_____

_____

_____

Of the six descriptive phrases in Revelation 13:1, which makes you most wonder if it refers to America? Why?

_____

_____

_____

_____

_____

_____

_____

How might it be conceivable that Americans would tolerate a satanic regime ruling over them?

_____

_____

_____

_____

_____

_____

If the beast in Revelation 13 is in fact America, describe what your emotional response would be.

_____

_____

_____

_____

_____

_____

_____

_____

_____

_____

_____

_____

CHAPTER TEN

THE WOUND THAT HEALED

As John continues to describe this superpower in the last days, he references animals, as Daniel did. **"The beast I saw resembled a leopard, but had feet like those of a bear and a mouth like that of a lion. The dragon gave the beast his power and his throne and great authority"** (Revelation 13:2). Daniel used a lion to describe the Babylonian Empire's power. It adds an element of pride, for which the Babylonians were noted. A bear symbolized the Media-Persian Empire, showing its brute force. A leopard represented the Greek Empire of Alexander the Great, emphasizing its strength and quickness. John, however, utilizes all three of these animals to describe the superpower of the last days, indicating how great it is compared to these others.

"The dragon gave the beast his power and his throne and great authority." We saw in Revelation 12:9 that the dragon is Satan himself. Recall that the kingdom Satan rules is the kingdom of the world, or society. For Satan to give his power and authority over his throne of the world would be to enable that superpower to gain the <u>number-one position</u> in all those elements that make up a society: economics, military strength, politics, industry, agriculture, production of goods and services, entertainment and so on.

We learn from the Book of Job that Satan's authority over the world is limited by God's providential guidelines. But overall, the worldly systems developed by unregenerate man are controlled or influenced by Satan and are often used to attack God's people in spiritual warfare. It is why we're told not to love the world, be friends of the world, or be polluted by it (James 4:4, 1 John 2:15, James 1:27). It is why we're to put on the armor of God to oppose the powers of this dark world (Ephesians 6:10-12); and to no longer conform to the pattern of this world, but have our minds renewed, for then we will be able to test and approve of what is God's will (Romans 12:2).

After World War II, the U.S. emerged as the most prosperous and mighty of all nations. This world conflict left the nations of Europe and the Pacific Rim in shambles. Many people lost not only their homes but their means of livelihood as well. The fighting destroyed factories, businesses, power plants, roads, bridges, rail lines and much more. Germany, England, France, Japan, Russia and other nations lost much of their industrial capacity. The infrastructure needed for economic productivity was wiped out by the war.

Consequently, the economic strength of these countries suffered a severe setback. England's financial and political power, for example, never regained its previous position. It went from being an industrial power with worldwide interests to a more internally focused nation with only a moderate role in international affairs. While the European and Pacific powers crawled out from under the rubble of the war, the U.S. was well on its way to economic supremacy. The war actually enhanced America's overall position.

None of the fighting occurred on American soil, so we emerged as the only major power with its industrial and agricultural base intact. This brought the development of a lifestyle that was previously unimaginable. After the fighting, production by American factories continued at a steady clip. We were uniquely able to furnish our wartime allies and enemies with products and services they needed. This allowed the average U.S. worker to have a steady job and good income. Few countries in the industrial world could boast higher pay, more extensive fringe benefits or better working conditions.

In the years after World War II, American products achieved a worldwide reputation. Our companies captured first place in the production of automobiles, machine tools, electronic equipment and other vital industries. Our output of quality agricultural goods was unsurpassed. We provided the majority of the goods and services needed elsewhere. This created an impressive trade surplus. Year after year, Americans sold far more overseas than they bought, and billions of excess dollars poured into the U.S. economy. One could say we were the emerging "great society."

As a result, the nation's standard of living went through the roof. The average American family claimed unprecedented worldly possessions. With less that 7% of the world's population, we held half of the world's wealth and were responsible for a third of the world's total yearly consumption of resources. From a material standpoint, Americans lived better than virtually all other people. This was not our position prior to the war.

AFTER WORLD WAR II, THE U.S. EMERGED AS THE MOST PROSPEROUS AND MIGHTY OF ALL NATIONS.

Soon the American lifestyle became the envy of people everywhere as we routinely enjoyed products and services completely out of reach for people in other lands. We emerged as the greatest political, military, industrial and economic power ever to exist. Indeed, it was like we had received the throne of the world, as John prophesied. This was soon proven as many countries aligned themselves with the United States government. The entire world was awestruck by the way the United States demonstrated its great power and ended the war with the dropping of the atomic bomb.

I am not condemning the way our economy flourished after World War II. I review our economic development because it relates to the materialistic lifestyle and spiritual warfare that has caused so much defeat for Christians in recent decades. I am grateful for the many conveniences, opportunities and freedoms we have. But these blessings make it easy to become attached to material things. The enemy's traps can be laid quite cleverly.

I have been successful in my career. However, the Lord tested us to expose the degree of our attachment to materialism. To be obedient to His guidance for our family, I had to give up my career and our material possessions. We were led by the Lord to remove our children from the humanistic philosophy being taught in the public-school system and to put them under Christian teachers in an environment consistent with that of our home. The verse the Lord used to confirm this directive was **"Blessed is the man who does not walk in the counsel of the wicked or stand in the way of sinners or sit in the seat of mockers. But his delight is in the law of the Lord, and on his law he mediates day and night"** (Psalms 1:1-2). We are to train our children in the way they should go, so that when they are old they will not turn from it (see Proverbs 22:6).

To obey the Lord's leading required selling the new house we built for our expanded family. It was on 15 acres of land with woods, a small flowing stream, a one-acre garden, and plenty of room for the kids to roam. It had become a favorite place for many of the activities for the church we attended. Even so, we had an auction, packed up our remaining things in two U-Haul trucks, and like a caravan began our 2000-mile cross-country journey to Phoenix where the Lord had directed us to move. There we found excellent Christian schools. Though finances were tight for the next several years as I began a new career, we kept the children in Christian schools. Another leading from the Lord in 1974 led my wife and I to found Paradise Valley Christian School (K-8), which is now one of the major Christian schools in the Phoenix area (visit the Web site, www.ParadiseValley-Christian.org).

The Lord has been faithful to our obedience. We now have 62 in our family, including children and spouses, grandchildren and great-grandchildren. Every one of them, except those who are still too young, has made a commitment to serve the Lord. Our testimony is that we have not experienced the normal drug, alcohol or divorce problems in a society where these have become all too common, even in Christian families. We are close-knit as the family stays in touch with each other, and gathers for holidays and special times.

A Major Identifying Event

John continues in Revelation 13:3 by prophesying about a major event in the history of this superpower's development—recovery from a mortal wound. **"One of the heads of the beast [superpower] seemed to have had a fatal wound, but the fatal wound had been healed. The whole world was astonished and followed the beast"** (Revelation 13:3). John says four things about this monumental event in the history of this superpower:

1. One of the heads of the "beast" (one area of the superpower's leadership) receives what appears to be a fatal wound. One aspect of its superiority is nearly wiped out. In Revelation 13:1, John said this superpower had *seven* heads—complete leadership in all areas of worldly influence. It is important to point out that only <u>one</u> *of the heads of the beast seemed to have had a fatal wound*, <u>not all seven</u>. John does not tell us in this verse which head suffered the wound and then recovered. He does, however, in verse 14. The second half of Revelation 13:14 reads, **"in honor of the beast who was wounded by the sword and yet lived."** In biblical times the phrase "by the sword" indicated military action. The wound was to this superpower's military head, and it appeared to be fatal.

2. This superpower's military leadership recovers from the blow. The wound heals.

3. The world is amazed by this. The recovery is dramatic, awesome and inexplicable. That is exactly what happened in World War II. In about 3 1/2 years we were victorious on two fronts, the European and Pacific. We ended the war with the dropping of the atomic bomb.

4. After the wound heals, the whole world is astonished at its recovery and follows this superpower. Following World War II, many

nations aligned themselves with our government and came under its influence. Our recovery catapulted us to a position of leadership in the world. As a superpower we grew as a direct result of our recovery from this near-fatal blow.

REVIEWING MILITARY HISTORY

For the American government to be the "beast" or superpower in Revelation 13, something in our country's past must match the description of a mortal wound. If we have become or are becoming this beast, then our military capability must have been severely crippled, after which we emerged on the world stage in such a dramatic turn of events that other nations were astonished.

> HISTORY UNCOVERS HOW CLOSE OUR INVOLVEMENT IN WORLD WAR II MATCHES JOHN'S PROPHECY.

The event *could not* have occurred within the last generation because we had already become a superpower by that time. And it must have been within the last century because at the time of the Civil War, Americans fought among themselves to decide whether there would even *be* an America. So the wound and the recovery occurred sometime during the first half of the 20th century.

Both World War I and II were watershed events for the U.S. However, it was after WWII that we truly became a superpower with global interests. Our influence in Africa, Asia, Europe and the Middle East continued to grow and expand during the Cold War era.

History uncovers an unnerving realization of how close the event that led to our involvement in World War II matches John's prophecy. This happened on December 7, 1941—the "day that will live in infamy." Probably few people today would equate Pearl Harbor with this prophecy. "Yes, it was horrible," they would say. "But a mortal wound?"

Because of its significance, and attempting to see if we fit all of the prophetic descriptions given about this last-days superpower, let's review that attack.

A Brief History of the Attack on Pearl Harbor

Historians, statesmen and journalists call this event one of the great turning points in world history. At the time, world leaders viewed this as a mortal wound to our military might. Prior to this, America had been reluctant to get involved in the war in Europe and Asia. But the Pearl Harbor attack jarred the United States into astonishing activity. It was the catalytic event of the century. As U.S. soldiers marched off to war, victory gardens sprang up, recycle bins appeared, and gas-rationing cards were used. Automobile factories were converted for jeep, tank and airplane production.

The Japanese attack on Pearl Harbor was sudden, spectacular and devastating. Congress convened a joint committee to investigate the event and filled 40 volumes with its findings. The Second World War transformed our land from a provincial, isolationist country to a technological hothouse of economic, political and military power.

To understand what happened at Pearl Harbor, and what led up to it, the book *At Dawn We Slept*, by Gordon W. Prange is considered by many to be the final word. His work has been praised as "a masterpiece," "authoritative," "unparalleled," "definitive" and "impossible to forget."

Prange was uniquely qualified for this writing task. He was educated at the University of Iowa and the University of Berlin. Later, he taught history at the University of Maryland. From 1946 to 1951, Prange was chief of General Douglas MacArthur's G-2 Historical Section located at General HQ, Far East Command, Tokyo.

From his firsthand knowledge, Prange knew more about the attack on Pearl Harbor than anyone else. He also interviewed virtually every surviving Japanese officer who took part in the operation, as well as every pertinent source on the U.S. side. His 873-page history of the attack is based on 37 years of research. His book was used as a major source in the making of *"Tora! Tora! Tora!"* the movie about Pearl Harbor.

Military historians agree that when the Japanese attacked Pearl Harbor, the United States suffered the greatest defeat any nation had ever endured at the beginning of a war. It is difficult to overstate the importance of naval power prior to the age of aviation. At the time, ships represented the ultimate in technological achievement. Battleships were the mightiest weapons of war, and luxury liners epitomized Western culture. When a great ship sank—the *Lusitania*, the *Bismarck* or the *Titanic*—people listened to the details in amazement. These events inspired legends, ballads and movies. Sinking ships were cataclysmic events akin to natural disasters like earthquakes and hurricanes. At Pearl Harbor, the United States had 22 ships either sunk or damaged in a matter of hours!

PRELUDE TO THE ATTACK

In the spring of 1940, a large segment of the U.S. Pacific Fleet was stationed at Pearl Harbor. It was the world's greatest aggregation of warships—a million tons of fighting steel. But the U.S. influence in the Pacific irritated the Japanese. While European nations fought each other in the 1930s, this island nation saw a golden opportunity to expand its empire into Southeast Asia. But Japan feared that our huge naval presence in the Pacific threatened their ambitious plans.

So in December 1940, Fleet Admiral Isoroku Yamamoto, Commander-in-Chief of the Combined Fleet of the Imperial Japanese Navy, convinced the Japanese Imperial Council to employ their aircraft carriers to launch a surprise attack at Pearl Harbor. He reasoned that for Japan to achieve political supremacy in the Pacific, it had to neutralize America's military capacity there.

Yamamoto's idea was to catch us sleeping—literally. He knew that just as a weaker judo expert can toss a stronger opponent by catching him off balance, Japan needed to seize the initiative. By striking a fatal blow in one bold attack, Yamamoto hoped to gain the military edge in the Pacific for a year. He and his advisors concluded that if Japan had that advantage, they could win in the Pacific against the United States.

His plan had merit! The majority of our people were caught completely off guard. A statement made on February 19, 1941, by Congressman Charles I. Faddis of Pennsylvania sums up the United States' perspective: *"The Japanese are not going to risk a fight with a first class nation. They are unprepared to do so, and no one knows better than they do. They will not dare to get into a position where they must face the American Navy in open battle. Their Navy is not strong enough and their homeland is too vulnerable."*

It took the Japanese forces a year of intense preparation. Planning had to be done in the strictest secrecy. If the attack did not catch the United States by surprise, it would fail. The Japanese faced several tactical problems. They had to design and build special torpedoes capable of operating in the shallow waters of Pearl Harbor; produce new armor-piercing shells that planes could deliver from low altitudes; select and train pilots how to fly in low and attack such an area; and organize a naval task force and teach the personnel how to refuel the ships in the rough seas of the north Pacific—the route chosen to avoid detection and assure complete surprise. The Pearl Harbor plan was the most highly classified, closely guarded secret of World War II prior to the Manhattan Project (our development of the atomic bomb).

At 6 o'clock on the morning of November 26, 1941, the Japanese strike force weighed anchor. Eleven days later, just before dawn on December 7, they reached the launching point for their attack: 230 miles due north of Oahu, Hawaii. The task force of 33 warships, including six aircraft carriers, had successfully sailed on a northern route through rough waters and dense fog to avoid detection by American ships and surveillance aircraft.

DAY OF INFAMY

The attack came that Sunday morning with startling swiftness. On every Japanese carrier, the scene was the same. The engines sputtered to life, up fluttered the signal flag and down again, as one by one the aircraft roared down the flight decks, drowning out the cheers and yells from the crews. Plane after plane rose in the sky, flashing in the early morning sun that peeked over the horizon. This airborne armada consisted of 353 planes. It represented the largest concentration of airpower in the history of warfare. On the peaceful target island, American sailors were unaware of the tremendous fighting force that would send many of them to a watery grave.

Perfect timing was essential. Our enemy knew full well that if anything went wrong, the entire attack would collapse. But they were dead on course. Their mission: destruction of the U.S. Pacific Fleet stationed at Pearl Harbor and all of the nearby Air Force installations.

It was 7:40 a.m. when the first Japanese pilots sighted Oahu's coastline. Mitsuo Fuchida, the Japanese commander who led the first formation of planes (and who became a Christian after the war), later wrote: *"The harbor was still asleep in the morning mist."* The element of surprise remained with the Japanese.

As the first wave of planes approached Pearl Harbor, they deployed into three groups. They first struck our air bases so our fighter planes could not counterattack the bombing. They hit Hickam Air Force Base, Wheeler Field, Bellows Field, Kaneohe Naval Base and the Naval Air Station at Ford Island. Japanese pilots flew in at treetop level, bringing massive destruction. Hangars were burned, barracks were razed, and hundreds of men were killed. A total of 341 U.S. planes were destroyed or damaged while still on the ground.

But the assault on the airfields was only the beginning. In the harbor were 96 warships of the United States Pacific Fleet. Included were 8 cruisers, 29 destroyers, 5 submarines, assorted minecraft and 8 U.S. battleships: the *West Virginia, Arizona, Oklahoma, Nevada, Tennessee, Pennsylvania, California* and *Maryland.*

At approximately 8:10 a.m. the battleship *USS Arizona* exploded, having been hit by a 1760-pound armor-piercing bomb. It slammed through her deck and ignited the main fuel tank. She sank in less than nine minutes. The *USS Oklahoma*, hit by several torpedoes, rolled completely over, trapping over 400 men inside. The *California* and *West*

Virginia sank at their moorings, while the *Utah*, which had been converted to a training ship, capsized with more than 50 of her crew. The *Maryland*, *Pennsylvania* and *Tennessee* all suffered significant damage. The *Nevada* tried to run out to sea but took several hits and had to be beached to avoid blocking the harbor entrance.

As the Japanese dive-bombers rocked the harbor, the mammoth gray ships along Battleship Row burned at their moorings, writhing from the explosions and sending billows of black smoke into the morning skies over Oahu. The Japanese dealt crippling blows to ship after ship. Most of the damage was done in the first fifteen minutes.

The attack on Pearl Harbor ended at about 9:45 a.m. In less than two hours the enemy had immobilized most of our air strength at Oahu and nearly eliminated their chief objective, the U.S. Pacific Fleet. A once-mighty military fortress had been pulverized. As the drone of enemy formations disappeared over the horizon, heading back to their carriers, they left behind a scene of horrible chaos—cackling flames, hissing steam and dying men. Half-submerged ships were strewn about the harbor, tilting at crazy angles. Wreckage floated across the oily surface of the water as bodies washed ashore.

As the billows of black smoke began to clear, U.S. forces assessed the damage. Twenty-two ships, including eight battleships, were sunk or heavily damaged. More than 340 American aircraft had been destroyed. Japanese losses totaled 29 aircraft destroyed and 74 damaged. In a couple of hours the enemy had secured mastery of the Far East. Historians write that America had suffered one of the greatest defeats any nation ever endured at the beginning of a war. In Germany, news of the defeat spurred Hitler to declare war on the United States.

THE FATAL WOUND IS HEALED

The attack seemed fatal, but it energized the fighting spirit of Americans as nothing else could have. Despite the wound that had cut the heart out of its military, the U.S. was soon to become the most fearsome warrior the world had ever known. During the next three and a half years, we forged a war machine that helped conquer enemy forces on two different fronts in the European and Asian theaters. America was transformed from a provincial, regional power to a technological, military and political titan stretching across both hemispheres. This in turn changed forever the American way of life.

The years have slipped by quickly, and most Americans have all but forgotten the scars of this attack. However, the grim reminder of defeat will live forever through the *Arizona* Memorial, dedicated on Memorial Day, 1962.

USS Arizona[1]

A single bomb sank the battleship *Arizona*. The bomb exploded in the main aviation fuel tank, and a tremendous internal chain reaction followed. The force of the explosion was so great it raised the bow of the ship completely out of the water and split her right behind the number-one gun turret. The *Arizona* sank in less than nine minutes. Out of her crew of 1543 men, 1177 lost their lives in those few awful minutes.

USS Arizona[1]

Today, the *USS Arizona* rests peacefully in an upright position under 38 feet of water at the bottom of Pearl Harbor. Oil still rises from her rusting hull, and the 1100 men still entombed there provide a silent but eloquent witness to the fury of Pearl Harbor Day.

Arizona Memorial Spans Sunken *USS Arizona*[1]

I was astounded to discover the theme used for building this memorial reflects the prophecy given by John in Revelation 13:3 when he said: **"One of the heads of the beast seemed to have had a fatal**

wound, but the fatal wound had been healed." The memorial was structurally designed with a sag in the middle to express our initial defeat—a wound to our military—but stands strong at the ends, expressing our recovery and victory.

Arizona Memorial Design[1]

After World War II, our country emerged as the greatest political, military, industrial and economic power in history. Many countries soon aligned themselves with the United States government. The entire world was awestruck by the way we demonstrated our great power and ended the war with the dropping of the atomic bomb. The fatal wound had indeed been healed.

---

[1] Photographs of the *USS Arizona* and the *USS Arizona* Memorial are assumed to be in the public domain. These images were reproduced for educational purposes. An unsuccessful attempt was made by the author to discover the identity of the photographers in order to credit them for their work.

Questions for Group Discussion and/or to Be Answered Individually

Many Americans today have no firsthand memory of Pearl Harbor. Prior to reading this book, how aware were you of what happened there?

_____

_____

_____

_____

_____

_____

Others have called this attack on Pearl Harbor one of the greatest turning points in world history. Do you agree or disagree? Why or why not?

_____

_____

_____

_____

Compare what took place at Pearl Harbor to what happened in our country on 9/11.

_____

_____

_____

_____

_____

_____

What are some of the major changes that have taken place in America since Pearl Harbor.

_____

_____

_____

_____

_____

_____

_____

Do you think this was the "fatal wound" John was referring to in Revelation 13:3? Why or why not?

_____

_____

_____

_____

_____

_____

Where are you now in your thinking about America possibly being the beast in Revelation 13?

_____

_____

_____

_____

_____

_____

CHAPTER ELEVEN

AMERICA IN PROPHECY CONTINUED

"**M**en worshiped the dragon because he had given authority to the beast, and they also worshiped the beast and asked, "Who can make war against him?"** (Revelation 13:4). In this verse the dragon has given his authority to the beast. Whether this takes place at a certain time or is more of an ongoing process, we are not told. There has definitely been a huge change taking place in our people of their commitment to Christian values during this last generation.

Worship means to serve, venerate or hold in awe. In this verse John describes the attitude of people on the Earth toward this last-days superpower. The question **"Who can make war against him?"** indicates unparalleled military might. John foretells that after this superpower recovers, it will demonstrate awesome military power, and command the respect and awe of peoples throughout the world.

The United States achieved this distinction on July 16, 1945, when scientists working near an old ranch house outside Alamogordo, New Mexico, detonated the first atomic bomb. At 5:30 a.m., American and exiled European scientists triggered humanity's first nuclear weapon. With a blinding flash of light, an intense heat and a massive shock wave roared past the observers as they watched a giant mushroom cloud rise above the desert.

On August 6, 1945, the B-29 bomber *Enola Gay* dropped an atomic bomb on Hiroshima, Japan. People and buildings became a black, boiling mass. Survivors wandered the streets in tattered clothes, crying out for water. Seventy thousand died in five minutes. Countless more perished from burns and cancer in the following months. Three days later, the U.S. dropped a second bomb on Nagasaki. Another 40,000 died instantly, with almost double that number dead within a year from radiation sickness. Japan surrendered unconditionally, asking only for the emperor to remain on his throne.

GOD REVEALED TO DANIEL THE SUPERPOWERS THAT WOULD HAVE A STRONG INFLUENCE ON THE PEOPLE OF ISRAEL.

Why President Truman decided to make the United States the only country to ever use a nuclear weapon during a war remains something of a mystery. Japan's war machine teetered on the brink of collapse; its factories idled for want of raw materials, its people starving on less than subsistence rations. Generals Marshall, Eisenhower and MacArthur believed nuclear weapons unnecessary. But one truth is clear: Americans exacted revenge on the Japanese for the earlier tragedy of Pearl Harbor. Now one country alone possessed the power to reduce entire cities to ashes, and all the other nations took notice. "America stands at this moment," said Winston Churchill in 1945, "at the summit of the world."

The attitude that prevailed after World War II—an attitude John prophetically calls worship or hold in awe—certainly describes the world's thinking after the defeat of Germany and Japan. Even today, regardless of what others think of the United States, they stand in awe of our lifestyle and our position of world leadership.

"The beast was given a mouth to utter proud words and blasphemies and to exercise his authority for forty-two months. He opened his mouth to blaspheme God and to slander his name and his dwelling place and those who live in heaven" (Revelation 13:5-6). To **"utter**

proud words" is to promote ourselves as better than others. We Americans have become a prosperous, powerful, profane and proud people, taking great pride in our worldly position, accomplishments and conquests. **"There are six things the Lord hates, seven that are detestable to him:** (these seven include) **haughty** (proud) **eyes, a lying tongue, hands that shed innocent blood"** (Proverbs 6:16-17). **"When pride comes, then comes disgrace, but with humility comes wisdom"** (Proverbs 11:2). There are many verses of Scripture that denounces pride.

"to exercise his authority for forty-two months." We have discussed that the Hebrew writers used a period of 1260 days, time, times and half a time, which forty-two months also equals, to state a period of time the Lord does not make known.

"to blaspheme God and to slander his name." In verse 2 we were told that this beast receives three worldly positions: 1. power: 2. throne of the world or of Satan's kingdom, which would mean we become the greatest superpower being number one in all areas of worldly affairs: 3. authority. While in this position we use the name of God irreverently in a way that misrepresents and injures His Holy name, which is blasphemy.

Before continuing our examination of Revelation 13, this is a good place to stop and look at what Daniel prophesied about this beast/superpower in the last days.

DANIEL AND THE END-TIMES BEAST/SUPERPOWER

Just as John did, Daniel also wrote of a "beast" with "ten horns" and a mouth that spoke boastfully. Could two men who lived centuries apart be describing the same vision? Yes and no. Both Daniel and John wrote about the last-days superpower, but from different reference points.

The Old Testament prophet had a dream (see Daniel 7) in which God revealed the empires from Daniel's day until the end of time that would have a strong influence on the people of Israel. Following the destruction of Jerusalem in A.D. 70, a great dispersion of the Jewish people took place. It was not until 1948 that the modern state of Israel came into existence. Therefore, Daniel would not have prophesied about empires between A.D. 70 and 1948, because Israel did not exist as a nation during that time. Therefore, his prophecy was of those beasts or superpowers before A.D. 70 and also the end-times superpower. It is also essential to understand that Daniel's prophecies centered on his people and those superpowers that helped shaped Israel's history.

"After that, in my vision at night I looked, and there before me was a fourth beast terrifying and frightening and very powerful. It had large iron teeth; it crushed and devoured its victims and trampled under foot whatever was left. It was different from all the former beasts, and it had ten horns" (Daniel 7:7).

In these verses, the ten-horned beast is similar to the one John saw; however, Daniel is not describing the same beast. Daniel wanted to know the identity of this fourth beast. Later in the same chapter, he receives his answer. **"The fourth beast is a fourth kingdom** (superpower) **that will appear on earth. It will be different from all the other kingdoms and will devour the whole earth, trampling it down and crushing it. The ten horns are ten kings who will come from this kingdom"** (Daniel 7:23-24a). Bible scholars generally agree that this "fourth beast" is the Roman Empire.

"While I was thinking about the horns, there before me was another horn, a little one, which came up among them; and three of the first horns were uprooted before it. This horn had eyes like the eyes of a man and a mouth that spoke boastfully" (Daniel 7:8). "Little horn" means a young or new nation. The little horn grew out of the ten horns but remained *distinct* or separate from them. Daniel prophesied of world empires in existence from his day until the end of time that greatly influenced Israel as a nation. This little horn, or nation, he introduces, which arises out of the countries from the Roman Empire, will be that superpower influencing Israel after she regains her position as a nation near the end of time. **We are that young nation** and have been the influential power over Israel since they regained their homeland in 1948.

This was explained to Daniel as follows: **"After them another king will arise, different from the earlier ones; he will subdue three kings. He will speak against the Most High and oppress his saints and try to change the set times and the laws. The saints will be handed over to him for a time, times and half a time"** (Daniel 7:24b-25).

DANIEL'S PROPHECY

Putting these interpretations together reveals a prophecy that unfolds like this:

1. Out of the Roman Empire emerges a bloc of prominent countries.
2. From this bloc comes a new country composed of people from the Roman Empire.
3. This new country defeats three of the other countries in order to achieve its separate status.
4. This new country gains power and influence greater than any of the countries from which its people came.
5. After reaching the status of a power with worldwide influence, this new country begins to turn on the saints.
6. Christians are worn down for an unknown period of **"time, times and a half time."**

These six points describe America quite well. Europe emerged from its position as the northern region of Rome's empire, and the United States came together from the peoples of Europe. We defeated three of the nations from the Roman Empire—England, France and Spain—in the development of our nation. We went on to become a superpower as a result of WWII, after which our government began to turn against the saints by changing the laws of its society. This is happening in our generation, through abortion, removing the name of God in government buildings and in the classroom, forbidding public prayer, lack of censorship in the electronic media, etc.

No other country even comes close to fulfilling these prophecies. America, barely 200 years old, became a superpower—the mightiest in world history. We have had a unique influence over the Jewish people, as prophesied by Daniel, and Christians, as prophesied by John. Both prophesy of this last superpower, and their approach is similar, but from different points of reference.

REVIVED ROMAN EMPIRE

The beast Daniel prophesied about is the ancient Roman Empire. The little horn is pictured as coming from it. Many scholars have described a resemblance between the old Roman Empire and contemporary American society. The two societies share common characteristics such as militarism, world commerce and hedonism. So similar are the two that a recent U.S. president commissioned a study to learn why Rome collapsed, so America might avoid the same demise.

> THE U.S. FULFILLS THE PROPHESIED REAPPEARANCE OF THE ROMAN EMPIRE.

The spirit of the revived Roman Empire bears a similarity to the fulfillment of a prophecy during the time of Jesus. When our Lord walked the Earth, Jewish scholars anticipated the reappearance of the prophet Elijah, because according to Old Testament he would precede the coming of the Messiah. Scripture tells us this prophecy was fulfilled through John the Baptist (Matthew 11:14, Luke 1:17) because his spirit was much like that of Elijah's. In this same way the U.S. fulfills the prophesied reappearance of the Roman Empire. The spirit that prevailed in pagan Rome now characterizes contemporary American society. And just as religious leaders in Jesus' day failed to recognize the fulfillment of the prophecy about Elijah, many Christians do not realize that we fulfill the description of the prophecy concerning the reviving of the ancient Roman Empire.

As we prepare for what's ahead the significance of Revelation 13:7-10 is such that I have allocated the entire next chapter to these verses. The rest of Revelation 13, verses 11 through 18, will be presented in this chapter.

A Second Beast

"Then I saw another beast, coming out of the earth; it had two horns like a lamb, but it spoke like a dragon" (Revelation 13:11). This second beast is subject to, and serves the interests of, the first beast. Like a lamb, appears harmless, but it insidiously represents and promotes perverted values (Daniel 7:25). This second beast has the appearance of a false prophet, proclaiming godly interests while teaching anti-Christian values. It is called a false prophet in Revelation 16:13, 19:20 and 20:10, and in that sense it represents the spirit of a religion prostituted for evil ends teaching false values and standards.

More specifically the teaching influence of values that developed through modern technology has become extremely powerful and dynamic. It cannot be denied, we are in a revolutionary cultural war for the hearts and minds of the American people and their lifestyle. Since WW II our government has occupied a central place in this unholy war against the saints in what can be called the greatest onslaught against American Christianity and its values since the birth of our nation.

There Is a Mind Behind the System

John identifies a spiritual force behind the corruption of America. This second beast orchestrates the transformation of this nation by means of a strategy intended to destroy the will of those who resist. The strategy is to permanently alter the way people think about social problems and personal actions.

The church has often depicted the beasts in Revelation as some kind of monstrosities. One of the oldest literary devices is to make good things beautiful and evil things ugly. In the fairy tales we learned as children, bad things were represented by monsters, hags and ogres, while good things were portrayed by handsome princes and fair maidens. Artists use a scaly, horned figure with a tail to depict the devil, yet Scripture reveals that he appears **"as an angel of light"** (2 Corinthians 11:14). As John prophetically describes in Revelation 13:11, the teaching power of our society may appear harmless (like a lamb), but the spirit being taught (spoke like a dragon) once the first beast comes to power, will be a continuance of anti-Christ characteristics centered in serving self.

American society has perfected many characteristics of the world giving it great power to tempt Christians to step outside of God's Word becoming preoccupied with serving self; my well being, my pleasures, my desires, my ambitions, deciding for myself right verses wrong.

"It [the second beast] **exercises all the authority of the first beast in its presence, and makes the earth and its inhabitants worship the first beast, whose mortal wound had been healed. It works great signs, even making fire come down from heaven to earth in the sight of men; and by the signs which it is allowed to work in the presence of the beast, it deceives those who dwell on earth, bidding them make an image for the beast which was wounded by the sword and yet lived; and it was allowed to give breath to the image of the beast so that the image of the beast should even speak, and to cause those who would not worship the image of the beast to be slain. Also it causes all, both small and great, both rich and poor, both free and slave, to be marked on the right hand or the forehead, so that no one can buy or sell unless he has the mark, that is, the name of the beast or the number of its name"** (Revelation 13:12-17, RSV).

In the past, great empires relied on military might to control other countries. They would plunder the goods of the people and oftentimes tax them heavily. Even in modern times, communism ruled through the barrel of a gun. But the beast superpower of Revelation 13 uses a different method to influence and dominate people. It rules through the technological power of its society.

Since World War II, our tremendous advancement in world leadership has primarily been the outgrowth of our electronic technology.

Most of these developments we take for granted and consider commonplace, but John from his perspective describes what he saw as great and miraculous signs. There is nothing inherently wrong with electronic technology. It is a part of God's creation; electricity is used for many wonderful things. But Satan controls the world; therefore, many of the wonders electricity makes possible are going to be primarily part of his system. For example, television provides a direct means of mind control that appears harmless, but deceives because it overdevelops the sense of serving self. Anything that has the ability to plant thoughts in our minds is a teacher and a potential deceiver.

The creation of electronic media has allowed Satan to capture human imagination as never before. It has provided him with teaching influence for every minute of every hour of every day. The idea hardly exists any more that there should be time and space reserved for family life. By far the largest exporter of TV programming, we impact people around the world with our immoral lifestyle, presenting our often-perverse values through the power of the second beast.

AN IMAGE

John states that our society will fashion an "image" for the first beast. Since our main source of power has been developed through the technology of electronics, it would be logical that the image would be an electronic one. The Greek word used for "image" is *eikon*, which means "representation" or "manifestation." So the second beast crafts an *eikon* of the first beast, and this image is used **"so that no one could buy or sell unless he has the mark"** (Revelation 13:17). John's prophetic language is not as incomprehensible as it may seem. He is saying that out of our society there will be a product developed that gives the government the ability to control the commercial activities (the buying and selling) of its citizens.

Consistent with the description given by John's prophecy, it appears this image has already been developed—the computer. No machine in history matches its influence. Since World War II, this amazing device has become part of every facet of public and private life. Computers perform such an astonishing array of activities that modern life would be impossible without them. They possess a powerful technological brain—the microchip.

COMPUTERS READ MARKS NOT NUMBERS!

The entire world of commerce and industry now functions by use of computers. Transportation relies on computers for everything from navigation to the scheduling of maintenance. Medicine uses them to diagnose illnesses and to fill prescriptions to cure them. Department stores, banks, hospitals, utilities, post offices, universities, industry, etc.—every modern institution functions by means of computer technology. The electronic computer is truly an image, or representation and manifestation, of a human creation using modern-day technology that fulfills John's prophecy.

I know little about computers. It is not difficult to see, however, that the harnessing of the Earth's electromagnetic force of electricity, which a few hundred years ago was just lightning in the sky, has resulted in devices capable of performing complex human activities, including reproduction of the human voice. This fits John's references of the second beast's ability to make fire come down from Heaven and to give breath to the image of the first beast so it could speak. Several years ago *Time* magazine, January 3, 1983, announced its 1982 "Man of the Year" was not a man, but the computer.

"Also it causes all, both small and great, both rich and poor, both free and slave, to be marked on the right hand or the forehead, so that no one can buy or sell unless he has the mark" (Revelation 13:16-17a, RSV). In the future it will be necessary for the superpower to control economic transactions. I don't know what all these commercial regulations will entail, but some kind of system will be imposed. A marking system of the kind John describes has already been developed. It is found on practically every item in almost any store. It is called the Universal Product Code, which looks like a series of vertical lines or marks covering an area the size of a large postage stamp. The UPC-symbol technology has been in use in our country since 1973. Computers read marks not numbers!

Although the barcodes on grocery items are the most noticeable, credit and bank cards also use barcodes. These are micro-encoded along the magnetic strip on the back of the card. When these marks are scanned by laser light, the optical pattern is converted to an electrical signal (analog), converted to a digital signal, and decoded by a microprocessor. Literally tens of thousands of characters can be micro-encoded on the 3" × 0.5" magnetic strip on a single card. It is possible to record a personal record of every person's purchases, transactions, and so on.

So when do I think our system of economic control will unfold? I don't know! The technology for a cashless society already exists. Credit cards make the introduction of a national ID card possible right now. In addition, existing technology could be used to implant information beneath the skin on the head, arm or other place on the body, and new technology is constantly being introduced. The manipulation for using such technology for social control might follow a major social or political event, appear in the aftermath of a natural disaster, or result from the fallout of a major economic shake-up.

HEAVY DEBT

I am not an economic whiz, but it is not difficult to understand economists' warning that the heavy debt we have incurred over the last 15-20 years will someday have to be paid back. For some, this is a matter of greed. They already have more than most people in the world, but still are not satisfied. However, for most Americans, indebtedness is a matter of ignoring economic reality. We have grown accustomed to the material possessions that make up what we call "the good life." Few seem to realize they have become victims of a worldly deception that ensnares people through irresistible advertising and product availability.

We have been led to expect a lifestyle that is getting harder and harder to achieve. Therefore, the widening gap between expectations and capabilities has created a nearly irresistible dependence on credit. Buying on credit is the only way for many Americans to get what we now think of as our birthright. Few understand the reality of our nation's economic position in comparison to the rest of the world. Personal debt has reached a record high; savings, an all-time low. Government is in the same boat. Cities, states and the federal government must borrow in order to maintain public services. Credit has put a stranglehold on our economy.

We have dug ourselves into an economic black hole. During the 1980s, our country shifted from being the largest creditor nation in the world to being the largest debtor nation. People face huge personal debt. Corporations juggle massive business debt. Government operates with gigantic deficits.

Because we supplied the rest of the world with many of its goods and services after World War II, when other countries lost their industrial infrastructure, dollars poured into our country. America developed an unheard-of standard of living. That was not the case before World War II. In recent years we have maintained this living standard through credit. The insurmountable debt that has resulted does not look good.

Few politicians and corporate chieftains seem willing to admit this, but our years of subconscious overspending cannot be eradicated. No matter what the politicians promise, record indebtedness could ultimately result in financial judgment.

In a larger sense, what the government does or doesn't do at this point won't make much difference. Current "solutions" to the debt crisis amount to economic fiction rather than sound thinking. Take the idea of consumer spending, which says the economy will be healthy as long as consumer spending remains strong. In other words, everybody will be poorer unless people spend more than they can afford. That just doesn't make sense!

Many economists predict there is no way to spend our way out of this dilemma—that is the bottom line. Whether consumers spend more, or spend less; whether the government taxes more, or taxes less, the debt will continue to grow. Traditional methods to prop up the economy simply are not feasible. No conventional solutions are available, because this is an unheard-of economic problem.

The "spirit of merchandising" has grabbed people's hearts, and many American families now depend on two incomes to meet their obligations. The loss of one income even for a brief period would tilt them dangerously close to financial ruin. At the root of this vulnerability is our failure to live within our means. Consumer debt, corporate debt and government debt have all risen in a vain effort to maintain our present standard of living. We have mortgaged the future to pay for the present.

At some stage we will reach that critical point where the rising debt collides with falling earnings. When the right portion of

ECONOMISTS PREDICT THERE IS NO WAY TO SPEND OUR WAY OUT OF THIS DILEMMA.

debt goes unpaid, the credit system that drives our economy will falter. What will break the camel's back—the shock that will trigger a major economic change—is unknown at the time I write this book, but God's prophetic Word declares it will happen.

There might be significant social and political fallout to a major economic catastrophe. A major financial panic could bring civil disorder, violence and unimaginable chaos, not necessarily because Americans will lack basic necessities, but because we will be denied the things we want. This is not the same as it was during the Great Depression. During the 1930s, the majority of people were accustomed to working hard for simple necessities. The generation that survived the Depression was glad to have enough to eat, something to wear, and a roof over their heads. But our self-centered, materialistic, technology-dependent generation will not be content with that.

If this should happen, few Americans will resist government intervention; in fact, many will probably demand it. It will open the door that will give our government great incentive to eliminate perceived threats to the economy by extending control over buying and selling. It would be easy for government leaders of the beast-system to promise social order in return for absolute compliance.

It is difficult to say what these commercial regulations will entail, but Bible prophecy points to a day when our superpower government will control economic transactions. A marking system of some kind will be imposed as John prophesied, **"so that no one could buy or sell unless he has the mark, that is, the name of the beast or the number of its name"** (Revelation 13:17, RSV). John tied the marking system with the numbering system of the beast society as the method used for control. Only by the wisdom of God could he have known our modern day marking system used by computers.

"This calls for wisdom: let him who has understanding reckon the number of the beast, for it is a human number, its number is six hundred and sixty-six" (Revelation 13:18, RSV). The number six throughout Scripture is the number of man—his doings, comings and goings. The fact the Lord used three 6's in closing out this prophecy is something that needs to be considered when seeking application. Let me give you something to ponder.

The make-up of a human being consists of three parts: body, mind and spirit. The number of man in Scripture is 6. Three 6's would indicate the whole of man; all three parts. According to this prophecy, a time is coming when the beast-system will implement the control of buying and selling by requiring people to receive a physical mark. The reason why we would be open to receive this mark is because of our strong desire to serve ourselves, a condition that has already captured the hearts of many in our country. It is an anti-Christ spiritual condition that the enemy has been able to work through the beast-system to constantly tempt us to serve ourselves over and above what is normal. This causes us to oppose the laws of God by setting ourselves up in the temple of God, in Christianity human beings are the temple of God, so that we can serve ourselves as if we were a god. That is how the beast-system has been using deception to overcome the saints.

LIVING WITHIN THE BEAST-SYSTEM

We are to live in the physical world, even though we are no longer a member of its spiritual kingdom. We were bought at a price, reborn spiritually, and are now members of God's Kingdom to be the **salt of the earth** and the **light of the world**. So what, specifically, is the responsible attitude Christians should have living under the beast-system?

The answer is found in the Book of Romans where Paul instructs Christians living under the Roman Empire, which also was called a beast in prophetic Scriptures. In the first seven verses of Romans chapter 13, Paul explains the nature of Christian's citizenship in this world. He did not teach believers to be anarchists or to revolt. He taught those who feared God to respect the institution of government. This principle of respect applies to all governments. **"Everyone must submit himself to the governing authorities,"** Paul writes, **"for there is no authority except that which God has established"** (Romans 13:1).

I understand the difficulty of respecting a government that performs its God-ordained mission poorly. Since our government "gained the throne of the world" after World War II as John prophesied (Revelation 13:2), it has allowed the spirit of lawlessness to grow. American society has also become more violent and warlike. Our government has failed its God-ordained responsibility to maintain order.

Nevertheless, Paul says, Christians must not contribute to this disorder. **"He who rebels against the authority is rebelling against what God has instituted, and those who do so will bring judgment on themselves"** (Romans 13:2). Government, no matter how bad, is not necessarily a warning of bad news for those who fear God. Government is **"God's servant, an agent of wrath to bring punishment on the wrongdoer"** (Romans 13:4), and Christians must **"submit to the authorities, not only because of possible punishment but also because of**

conscience" (Romans 13:5). Only if we are told to deny the Lord should we take a stand, and even then, not with a rebellious attitude.

Christians are to live in a law-abiding, respectful and cooperative manner. The ideal Christian concept of citizenship is to be a model subject. **"Give everyone what you owe him: If you owe taxes, pay taxes; if revenue, then revenue; if respect, then respect; if honor, then honor"** (Romans 13:7). It is much easier to criticize this nation's leaders than to pray for them, but praying for them is what believers must do. **"I urge, then, first of all, that requests, prayers, intercession and thanksgiving be made for everyone—for kings and all those in authority, that we may live peaceful and quiet lives in all godliness and holiness"** (1 Timothy 2:1-2).

The church needs to prepare its people, young and old alike, to stand for Christ, even as it becomes more and more obvious what is happening. This is a spiritual truth that will set you free from the bondage of our world system that has spiritually imprisoned so many Christians.

QUESTIONS FOR GROUP DISCUSSION AND/OR
TO BE ANSWERED INDIVIDUALLY

Compare the two beasts John writes about in Revelation 13.

_____

_____

_____

_____

_____

_____

_____

How did Daniel's prophetic perspective differ from John's?

_____

_____

_____

_____

_____

_____

In what ways can it be fairly stated that America resembles the empire of ancient Rome?

_____

_____

_____

_____

_____

_____

_____

Past generations had a hard time picturing the "mark of the beast." What has changed in recent years that make this Scripture easier to imagine?

_____

_____

_____

_____

_____

_____

As a Christian, what practical steps can you take in order to have a greater impact for Christ in America? What should your response be in terms of the way you live?

_____

_____

_____

_____

_____

_____

Where has this chapter left you, emotionally speaking?

_____

_____

_____

_____

_____

_____

CHAPTER TWELVE

PATIENT ENDURANCE AND FAITHFULNESS

No one likes being blindsided.

Fights are bad enough to begin with. Hitting someone when they least expect it is cowardly.

Part of the reason Americans were so enraged in their response to Pearl Harbor was that at the very time the Japanese planes were completing their mission, two envoys from Tokyo were carrying on the pretense of diplomatic negotiations with the U.S. Secretary of State, Cordell Hull.

To ensure Satan will not catch God's people by surprise, Jesus gave John a message that informed them about what to expect. What He said was not always comforting, but the bottom line was that He would be triumphant, and faithfulness to Him would be rewarded.

"And I saw an angel coming down out of heaven, having the key to the Abyss and holding in his hand a great chain. He seized the dragon, that ancient serpent, who is the devil, or Satan, and bound him for a thousand years" (Revelation 20:1-2).

"And I saw the souls of those who had been beheaded because of their testimony for Jesus and because of the word of God. They had not worshiped the beast or his image and had not received his mark on their foreheads or their hands. They came to life and reigned with Christ a thousand years" (Revelation 20:4).

That's the good news. The bad news is that before these positive events take place, there is a time of intense spiritual warfare in these last days, which in addition to deception will include persecution. In His Olivet Discourse, Jesus says: **"Those will be days of distress unequaled from the beginning, when God created the world, until now—and never to be equaled again. If the Lord had not cut short those days, no one would survive. But for the sake of the elect, whom he has chosen, he has shortened them"** (Mark 13:19-20).

WHAT'S HAPPENED

We return to discuss those verses of Revelation 13, which we left out earlier, verses 7-10. The picture presented in Revelation 13 about the enemy's end-time spiritual warfare includes both deception and persecution. Verse 7 is a stern and important warning to everyone living in these last days. It reads, **"Also it** (the beast or superpower) **was allowed to make war on the saints and to conquer** (overcome) **them"** (Revelation 13:7a RSV).

The word **conquer** as used in this verse brings to mind to defeat or subdue, like one army by another, but not to obliterate or eliminate; much like what we did to Germany and Japan in WW II. This verse refers not only to the physical state of the saints in these last days, but also the spiritual. Recall Dr. Billy Graham stated a few years ago that his research concluded 90% of American Christians are living defeated spiritual lives. We may know what to say in Christian circles, but our actions or fruit has been broadcasting our weakness to the world and its standards. That is deception.

> VERSE 7 IS A STERN WARNING TO EVERYONE IN THESE LAST DAYS.

Deception is a terrible thing! One of the greatest warnings Jesus gave us about the last days was about deception. He said, **"For false Christs and false prophets will appear and perform great signs and miracles to deceive even the elect—if that were possible"** (Matthew 24:24).

We have spent considerable time discussing deception. Remember deception is determined by the fruit produced as compared to the teachings in the Word of God. The fruit in recent years produced by our society is the true barometer of our deception. This deception is a result of the overpowering ability our society has developed to influence and teach us its humanistic values and lifestyle.

There are other Scriptures in addition to John's prophecy in Revelation 13 that prophesy the saints will be conquered or overcome in these last days. We looked at the prophecy of Jesus in an earlier chapter comparing our day to the days of Noah. Another is Paul calling these last days terrible in II Timothy 3:1-5. He prophesied of the many worldly characteristics that would be evident in Christians. Speaking of Christians he said, **"But mark this: There will be terrible times in the last days. People will be lovers of themselves, lovers of money, boastful, proud, abusive, disobedient to parents, ungrateful, unholy** (immoral), **without love, unforgiving, slanderous, without self-control, brutal, not lovers of the good, treacherous, rash, conceited, lovers of pleasure rather than lovers of God—having a form of godliness but denying its power. Have nothing to do with them"** (II Timothy 3:1-5).

II Thessalonians chapter 2 is another prophecy about how the saints will be conquered or overcome in these last days. **"Concerning the coming of our Lord Jesus Christ and our being gathered to him, we ask you, brothers, not to become easily unsettled or alarmed by some prophecy, report or letter supposed to have come from us, saying that the day of the Lord has already come. Don't let anyone deceive you in any way, for that day will not come until the rebellion occurs and the man of lawlessness is revealed, the man doomed to destruction. He opposes and exalts himself over everything that is called God or is worshiped, and even sets himself up in God's temple, proclaiming himself to be God"** (II Thessalonians 2:1-4).

The first two verses we learn this prophecy is referring to the last days as it refers to the second coming of Jesus. Verse three proclaims a rebellion will occur. The Greek word Paul used for rebellion in this prophecy is *apostasia*. It means there will be a defection or falling away near the second coming of Jesus from following many of the standards of biblical Christianity.

I found verse 4 to be very revealing. **"He opposes and exalts himself over everything that is called God or is worshiped, and even sets himself up in God's temple, proclaiming himself to be God."** It describes the spirit of anti-Christ that will cause the rebellion or falling away, Christians being conquered in these last days.

The common teaching of this verse is the word temple refers to the temple in Jerusalem and that is possible. For that to happen however, the temple must be rebuilt and at the time of this writing the temple area is controlled by the Arabs and a Muslim mosque stands there.

IN CHRISTIANITY THE WORD TEMPLE REFERS TO THE HUMAN BODY.

Knowing that Paul was writing to Christians and in Christianity the word temple refers to the human body I did a word study on the word temple used in this verse. I believe it is important to share what I found.

Two different Greek words are used in Scripture for temple. One is *hieron,* which refers to the entire temple building. The other is *naos,* which is used for the inner sanctuary of the temple where the priests could enter. In Christianity Christians are the temple of God as everyone born again receives the gift of the Holy Spirit (see Acts 2:38). That is one of the key distinctions between Christianity and all other religions past or present. Every verse that teaches Christians become the temple of God the Greek word used for temple is *naos.* For example, **"Don't you know that you yourselves are God's temple (Greek word *naos*) and that God's Spirit lives in you?"** (I Corinthians 3:16). There are other verses that teach this and they too use the Greek word *naos* for temple. Jesus also used the Greek word *naos* in John 2:19-21 when he told the people that if they destroyed this temple, referring to His body, that He would raise it in three days.

I share this because in II Thessalonians 2:4 Paul used the Greek word *naos* for temple, not *hieron*. As he is discussing Christianity and the falling away in the last days, could this prophecy be referring to the human body too? This verse is a good definition of the religion of humanism and the new age movement. It has swept through our country in recent years and has been the major cause for the rapid deterioration of our country's moral values, and why many Christians have fallen into deception and no longer are committed to biblical standards. Humanism is to set ourselves up in the temple of God (*naos*—the human body) and decide right and wrong ourselves as though we were God. It has become the philosophy that is taught in most of our public schools and is used to establish the standards by which the majority of American people now live. Verse 4 prophesies this anti-Christ spirit will be the cause of the—*apostasia*—falling away.

I would also ask that you reflect back on our discussion in chapter five of the general characteristics of the Kingdom of God that are to be developed in all Christians. These characteristics are: Poor in spirit, mourning, meekness, to hunger and thirst for righteousness, to be merciful, pure in heart and peacemaker. Evaluate where you are in these characteristics becoming the image of your character. I think most of us would admit that our culture in recent years makes the development of these characteristics difficult.

Satan knows mankind's greatest weakness is to serve "self." It is a part of our sinful nature. As he observes the strength of God's people in any area, he strikes out against God by maneuvering his worldly systems to attack. This will probably be more direct and obvious someday through persecution. However, for today in America he is using deception. He dangles an overpowering temptation to serve the flesh by getting us to use our own reasoning to determine right and wrong. Since America gained the throne of the world after World War II, Satan has used this strategy, and he has been incredibly successful. This has resulted in the moral values of our country deteriorating more in this last generation than in all the years combined since we became a nation.

We have also experienced the greatest, most rapid moral decline of any society in history.

In a society that has a strong Christian influence, and where persecution is not immediately possible, Satan uses his strong worldly influence to deceive those who serve the Lord. He parades all the things our society has developed that are so attractive, using professional advertising to promote them, and the electronic media to present them, beautiful malls in which to display them, and easy credit to pay for them. Satan makes these enticements difficult to resist.

Even if we don't believe Satan's unseen hand is the direct cause of these things, but simply our own selfishness and greed, the result is the same. When in our hearts the things of the world become more important than our commitment to serve the Lord, our spiritual power to function as salt and light is lost. We find ourselves yielding to temptation, and we start establishing our own standards of right and wrong, which is to take the place of God in our hearts.

Another major trap the enemy is using in America is sexual immorality. This has always been one of Satan's major ways to bring about defeat, even among spiritual leaders. It certainly has captured the minds of many American people, including many Christians. King David is an example, which most of us are familiar. Lust has reached an epidemic level in our society. The sexual permissiveness that is put before American people through TV, movies, books, the Internet, magazines and so on has destroyed biblical standards in the minds of all too many.

We need to realize that the degree to which we are being influenced by the spirit of Satan does not have to be expressed through some kind of devil worship. It can be, and usually is, expressed by the degree to which we serve ourselves by holding to standards of our own making rather than those of Scripture.

The late Dr. Bill Bright, founder of Campus Crusade for Christ, wrote in his book *The Coming Revival*:

America is under siege. Tens of millions of Americans seem ensnared by an evil mind-set. The evidence is everywhere we look.

Officials have fought vigorously to expel God from our schools. The Ten Commandments cannot even be placed on the walls of most classrooms.

Powerful forces within our country want to make it illegal to mention the name of Jesus, carry Bibles, display religious pictures, or wear Christian emblems in schools and in the workplace. They argue that to do so creates an "offensive environment of harassment."

As a nation, we have spent our way into a $3 trillion national debt. It is still climbing at an alarming rate, threatening to bankrupt our nation in the next few years.

In many instances, our state and local governments are accused of linking arms with organized crime by legalizing lotteries and gaming houses. They are joining the ranks of the largest gambling operators in the world.

Selfishness has become a hallmark of the people. Americans are growing more cynical and less compassionate. Their attitudes toward minorities, immigrants, and the poor have hardened.

THE CHURCH IS ASLEEP

And where is the Church? For the most part, it is asleep. Polluted with the desires and materialism of the world, she knows little about spiritual discipline and living the Spirit -filled life. She is complacent and at ease, thinking she has everything and is in need of nothing.

This picture is a mirror image of the churches at Ephesus and Laodicea portrayed in Revelation 2:1-7; 3:14-21, to whom the Lord spoke these sobering words:

"You have forsaken your first love. Remember the height from which you have fallen! Repent and do the things you did at first. If you do not repent, I will come to you and remove your lampstand from its place" (Revelation 2:4, 5).

"I know your deeds, that you are neither cold nor hot. I wish you were either one or the other! So, because you are lukewarm—neither hot nor cold—I am about to spit you out of my mouth. You say, 'I am rich; I have acquired wealth and do not need a thing. But you do not realize that you are wretched, pitiful, poor, blind and naked" (Revelation 3:15-17).

These pictures of America and the Church are but a few of the alarming snapshots of our nation. As I thumb through the pages of our national album, I cannot help but feel a sting of shame. Our great and God-blessed nation has forsaken its once solid foundation of biblical principles. And much of the Church is spiritually impotent—void of a vital, personal, and intimate walk with God. Having fallen into the cult of the comfortable, the Church, for the most part, is no longer a power to be reckoned with. It has largely lost the respect of the masses; it is often the object of ridicule.

… America is a great resource providing more money, technology, and manpower to help fulfill the Great Commission than all other countries combined. If the enemies of the gospel had their way, America would no longer be a great sending nation; Satan would take away all of our religious freedoms.

God does not tolerate sin. The Bible and history make this painfully clear. I believe God has given ancient Israel as an example of what will happen to the United States if we do not experience revival. He will continue to discipline us with all kinds of problems until we repent or until we are destroyed, as was ancient Israel because of her sin of disobedience.

The Lord sent all sorts of calamities upon Israel, trying to get her attention and cause her to repent: "And still you won't return to me," says the Lord. "Therefore I will bring upon you all these further evils I have spoken of. Prepare to meet your God in judgment, Israel. For you are dealing with the one who formed the mountains and made the winds, and knows your every thought. … Jehovah, the Lord, the Lord Almighty, is his name" (Amos 4:11-13, TLB).

God is calling the Church to rise up and lead the nation to repent and follow Him. Our only hope is a supernatural visit from God."

This completes a look at this most important warning given to us in Revelation 13:7 about being overcome in these last days. We will continue our study of those remaining verses in Revelation 13 that we have not examined! **And he** (the beast / superpower) **was given authority over every tribe, people, language and nation. All inhabitants of the**

earth will worship the beast—all whose names have not been written in the book of life belonging to the Lamb that was slain from the creation of the world" (Revelation 13:7b-8).

Throughout Scripture prophets often foretold of a condition or general state of affairs, even though the actual fulfillment to the fullest degree did not take place. Daniel, for example, wrote of empires that controlled the world, yet Babylon, Persia, Greece, and Rome controlled only a limited part of the Earth's topography. They influenced the mainstream of civilization; therefore, Daniel illustrated the power of these empires and their worldly influence of all peoples.

Clearly, America does not control every person on the globe. Yet we influence nations and peoples throughout the world through the authority of our leadership in world politics, economics, military, and industrial power. Inhabitants of remote places receive American foreign aid, products, and American visitors. They learn about our culture through music and electronic media. Countries without formal political ties cannot escape our foreign policy. We are somewhat like a giant; whether the giant walks, stands, sits, or lies down, others are affected. There is no question that the majority of people look at America and our lifestyle with awe, which is what the word worship means.

COULD PERSECUTION BE WHAT'S AHEAD

"He who has an ear, let him hear. If anyone is to go into captivity, into captivity he will go. If anyone is to be killed with the sword, with the sword he will be killed. This calls for patient endurance and faithfulness on the part of the saints" (Revelation 13:9-10). These two verses will complete our examination of all verses in Revelation 13.

Christians have always experienced terrible times of suffering for their faith. But for some, at least, there was always the hope of escape to another country. For example, in 1977, Anglican Bishop Festo Kivengere of Uganda was urged by his people to flee the country following the murder of Archbishop Janani Luwum by dictator Idi Amin's forces. The believers told Festo and his wife, "One bishop's death this weekend is enough for us."

Under the cover of night, the two made it on foot across a mountain pass to Rwanda. But in Revelation, Jesus lets us know that a day may come when there will no longer be a place to which His people can flee because of the beast's influence and authority. The persecution referred to in Revelation 13 is carried out under the providence of God. That's the reason for the words of Revelation 13:10, which reads: **"If anyone is to go into captivity, into captivity he will go. If anyone is to be killed with the sword, with the sword he will be killed."** This could also imply that any kind of armed resistance will be out of the question.

MARTYRS

Though the verse doesn't include the word "martyrdom," it is certainly another possibility. Martyrs are integral to Revelation. For example, chapter 6, vv. 9-11 reads: **"When he opened the fifth seal, I saw under the altar the souls of those who had been slain because of the word of God and the testimony they had maintained. They called out in a loud voice, "How long, Sovereign Lord, holy and true, until you judge the inhabitants of the earth and avenge our blood?" Then each of them was given a white robe, and they were told to wait a little longer, until the number of their fellow servants and brothers who were to be killed as they had been was completed."**

Chapter 7, vv. 13-17: **"Then one of the elders asked me, 'These in white robes—who are they, and where did they come from?' I answered, 'Sir, you know.' And he said, 'These are they who have come out of the great tribulation; they have washed their robes and made them white in the blood of the Lamb. Therefore, they are before the throne of God and serve him day and night in his temple; and he who sits on the throne will spread his tent over them. Never again will they hunger; never again will they thirst. The sun will not beat upon them, nor any scorching heat. For the Lamb at the center of the throne will be their shepherd; he will lead them to springs of living water. And God will wipe away every tear from their eyes.'"**

And Revelation 12, verse 11: **"They overcame him** [Satan] **by the blood of the Lamb and by the word of their testimony; they did not love their lives so much as to shrink from death."**

The church has always flourished during times when Christians have bravely chosen to die rather than deny their faith. My assumption, therefore, is that this future worldwide testimony of countless martyrs will also, for the first time in history, bring about a revival in all countries of the globe. Key to what happens will not be biblical preaching, but rather the silent suffering of the saints.

What will sustain the faithful won't be sermons they recall about the Prosperity Gospel, but rather, those teachings they were given about being faithful even during desperately hard times. It's Bible stories like Shadrach, Meshach and Abednego saying to King Nebuchadnezzar, **"If we are thrown into the blazing furnace, the God we serve is able to save us from it, and he will rescue us from your hand, O king. But even if he does not, we want you to know, O king, that we will not serve your gods or worship the image of gold you have set up"** (Daniel 3:17-18).

FAITHFULNESS AND ENDURANCE

Bible passages hidden in believers' hearts will be deeply appreciated. I'm referring to verses about faithfulness, like:

"Praise be to the LORD, for he showed his wonderful love to me. ... You heard my cry for mercy when I called to you for help. Love the LORD, all his saints! The LORD preserves the <u>faithful</u>. ... Be strong and take heart, all you who hope in the LORD" (Psalm 31:21-24).

"Do not be afraid of what you are about to suffer. I tell you, the devil will put some of you in prison to test you, and you will suffer persecution. ... <u>Be faithful</u>, even to the point of death, and I will give you the crown of life" (Revelation 2:10).

"But the fruit of the Spirit is love, joy, peace, patience, kindness, goodness, <u>faithfulness</u>, gentleness and self-control" (Galatians 5:22-23a).

"The living, the living—they praise you, as I am doing today; <u>fathers tell their children about your faithfulness</u>" (Isaiah 38:19).

Revelation 13:10 ends this paragraph about the war the beast makes on the saints: **"This calls for patient endurance and faithfulness on the part of the saints."** Verses about patient endurance that come to mind include:

"Rather, as servants of God we commend ourselves in every way: <u>in great endurance</u>; in troubles, hardships and distresses; in beatings, imprisonments and riots; in hard work, sleepless nights and hunger..."

That's Paul in 2 Corinthians 6:4-5. An even more powerful example is found in Hebrews 12:2-3... **"Let us fix our eyes on Jesus, the author and perfecter of our faith, who for the joy set before him <u>endured</u> the cross, scorning its shame, and sat down at the right hand of the throne of God. Consider him who <u>endured</u> such opposition from sinful men, so that you will not grow weary and lose heart."**

THE EXAMPLE OF OTHER COUNTRIES

As this generation of Americans has continued to be blessed with freedom and peace, brothers and sisters in Christ the world over have had to practice patient endurance and faithfulness. One illustration is hardly adequate to represent the whole, but let's return momentarily to Uganda, where the East African revival has been going on for decades.

Archbishop Janani Luwam will always be a hero to believers there. For his opposition to dictator Idi Amin, Luwam was imprisoned on charges that he was hiding weapons for an armed rebellion. The church knew this was false because it had affirmed from the beginning that it would never be involved in using force or weapons. Their belief was that evil had to be overcome by good.

In his book *Revolutionary Love*, Bishop Festo Kivengere (mentioned earlier in this chapter) describes the scene:

More than four thousand people walked, unintimidated, past Idi Amin's guards to pack St. Paul's Cathedral in Kampala on February 20.

They repeatedly sang the "Martyrs' Song," which had been sung by the young Ugandan martyrs in 1885. Those young lads had only recently come to know the Lord, but they loved Him so much that they could refuse the evil things demanded of them by King Mwanga. They died in the flames singing, "Oh that I had wings such as angels have, I would fly away to be with the Lord." They were given wings, and the singing of those thousands at the Memorial Service had wings too.

PATIENT ENDURANCE AND FAITHFULNESS WILL BECOME MORE THE ORDER OF THE DAY.

We have no way of estimating the fresh impetus given by the martyrdom of Luwum to the Body of Christ. In Heaven we will know. After the service in the cathedral, the crowd gathered outside around the little cemetery where a grave had been dug for Janani beside that of Bishop Hannington, the first bishop for Central Africa sent out from England to the young church in Uganda. He was martyred by the same king in the same year as the boys.

Our archbishop's grave was empty because we had been denied the body of our leader. Soldiers had taken it far north to his own village of Kitgum for burial, in order to avoid the embarrassment to Amin of the discovery that he had died by bullets, not by a car accident as was pretended. At the open grave, former Archbishop Erica Sabiti quoted the words of the angels at the empty tomb of Jesus, "He is not here, He is risen!" Instantly a song of Zion burst out with such power that "Glory, glory, hallelujah" was heard from that hilltop far into the city. (77-78)

Patient endurance and faithfulness will be needed as persecution becomes more the order of the day throughout the world. The big question is when this happens whether American believers will be prepared to stand with their brothers and sisters from such places as Afghanistan, Algeria, Azerbaijan, Bangladesh, Bhutan, China, Colombia, Cuba, Egypt, Ethiopia, India, Indonesia, Iran, Iraq, Laos, Libya, Morocco, Myanmar

(Burma), Nepal, Nigeria, North Korea, Pakistan, Qatar, Saudi Arabia, Somalia, Sri Lanka, Sudan, Syria, Tajikistan, Tibet, Tunisia, Turkey, Turkmenistan, Uzbekistan, Vietnam, Yemen and still more nations where Christians are already frequently persecuted.

The ministry "The Voice of the Martyrs" says this year an estimated 160,000 Christians will die at the hands of their oppressors, and more than 200 million will be arrested, tortured, beaten or jailed. That's equal to 2/3 of the present United States population. Did you know that in many countries it is illegal to own a Bible, share your faith, change your faith or allow children under 18 to attend a religious service?

This is in spite of the fact that the United Nations' "Universal Declaration of Human Rights," Article 10, reads: *Everyone has the right to freedom of thought, conscience and religion; this right includes freedom to change his religion or belief, and freedom, either alone or in community with others and in public or private, to manifest his religion or belief in teaching, practice, worship and observance.*

WHAT ABOUT AMERICA?

Most American Christians would agree that faithfulness and patient endurance are good qualities. In real life, however, people tend to resist being trained in these areas. Patient endurance means sticking in there even when the going gets tough. It often requires bearing pain or injury without yielding, tolerating suffering with fortitude.

Faithfulness involves being trustworthy in the performance of duty, standing by your promises or obligations. 1 Corinthians 4:2 reads: **"Now it is required that those who have been given a trust must prove faithful."**

In this country, people's attitudes tend to be more like, "I don't need this hassle. Treat me nice or I'm out of here." Often it's how they relate to God too.

The truth is, patient endurance and faithfulness are not lessons we're all that fond of, which doesn't bode well in terms of us being prepared if future hardships come.

Here is a simple prayer that could serve you well in preparing for the days ahead.

Lord, I give You permission to start teaching me about patient endurance and faithfulness. I know I am not as skilled in these matters as I should be. When You sense I have started to learn these lessons, I pray that You would also help me share them with those I love the most. Amen.

The time could come when justice and fair-mindedness is set aside for the will of tyrants and Jesus-haters. This ill treatment will not be something new. The world has already had more than its share of abuse of this kind. The only difference will be in its scope.

It will do no good to look to the courts to make things right. They will be under the control of the beast / superpower. The same will be true of the police and the military. The nightmare will be complete because, as impossible as it sounds, even some of the religious authorities will answer to the enemy.

Christians may be treated like outcasts. Justice for them may be difficult to achieve. To look for mercy could be an exercise in futility. It will not be found among the majority. There could be a time of great misery and sorrow for some of the saints, even in America.

But it won't last all that long.

In His time the rightful King will return in triumph.

"Then I saw a new heaven and a new earth, for the first heaven and the first earth had passed away, and there was no longer any sea. I saw the Holy City, the new Jerusalem, coming down out of heaven from God, prepared as a bride beautifully dressed for her husband. And I heard a loud voice from the throne saying, 'Now the dwelling of God is with men, and he will live with them. They will be his people, and God himself will be with them and be their God. He will wipe every tear from their eyes. There will be no more death or mourning or crying or pain, for the old order of things has passed away'" (Revelation 21:1-4).

QUESTIONS FOR GROUP DISCUSSION AND/OR TO BE ANSWERED INDIVIDUALLY

In America, is the society influencing the church more, or is the church influencing society more? Support your answer.

_____

_____

_____

_____

_____

_____

How prepared do you think American Christians are for persecution and martyrdom?

_____

_____

_____

_____

_____

What is your present level of concern for fellow Christians around the world who are facing persecution? How does knowing that many face persecution stir you to respond?

_____

_____

_____

_____

_____

Do you think you will make use of the suggested prayer about praying for persecution? Why or why not?

_____

_____

_____

_____

_____

_____

_____

Dr. Bill Bright's quote ends with a call to the church to "rise up and lead the nation to repent and follow Him (Jesus)." What is keeping the American church from doing this?

_____

_____

_____

_____

_____

_____

_____

If your commitment to Christ were the norm for all of today's believers in America, how would that bode for the future of our land?

_____

_____

_____

_____

_____

_____

_____

CHAPTER THIRTEEN

HOW THEN SHALL WE LIVE?

L iving in the last days, which most Christians believe, it is critical that we understand what God has told us about this period of time. We need to take heed and learn a lesson from the Jewish Nation who did not understand the prophetic Scriptures about their day and missed the incarnate, Jesus, when He came the first time. We have covered the prophetic Scriptures that warn us about the great deception that is taking place in our day. At some point the beast / superpower in Revelation 13 will also persecute believers. Senior Pastor Don Wilson at Christ Church of the Valley, Phoenix, AZ, one of the largest churches in America with attendance any given weekend of 12,000 to 15,000, stated from the pulpit April 5, 2009, *"...in the next 10 years, I believe I will probably go to jail in Phoenix for preaching the gospel."* The bottom line is, those who are wise will also prepare for that possibility. Prophetic Scriptures seem to indicate that persecution is going to happen, and probably sooner than later.

If these words sounds fatalistic, just read the next few chapters of Revelation and be glad you <u>aren't</u> numbered with those who bear the mark of the beast. In that case, what you have to look forward to are the seven terrible bowls of God's wrath (chapter 16) and the destruction of the capital city of the Antichrist, eschatological Babylon (chapters 17-18).

Then imagine yourself as a nonbeliever reading these terrifying verses!

"I saw heaven standing open and there before me was a white horse, whose rider is called Faithful and True. With justice he judges and makes war. His eyes are like blazing fire, and on his head are many crowns. He has a name written on him that no one knows but he himself. He is dressed in a robe dipped in blood, and his name is the Word of God. The armies of heaven were following him, riding on white horses and dressed in fine linen, white and clean. Out of his mouth comes a sharp sword with which to strike down the nations. 'He will rule them with an iron scepter.' He treads the winepress of the fury of the wrath of God Almighty. On his robe and on his thigh he has this name written: KING OF KINGS AND LORD OF LORDS.

"And I saw an angel standing in the sun, who cried in a loud voice to all the birds flying in midair, 'Come, gather together for the great supper of God, so that you may eat the flesh of kings, generals, and mighty men, of horses and their riders, and the flesh of all people, free and slave, small and great.'

"Then I saw the beast and the kings of the earth and their armies gathered together to make war against the rider on the horse and his army. But the beast was captured, and with him the false prophet who had performed the miraculous signs on his behalf. With these signs he had deluded those who had received the mark of the beast and worshiped his image. The two of them were thrown alive into the fiery lake of burning sulfur (destroyed). The rest of them were killed with the sword that came out of the mouth of the rider on the horse, and all the birds gorged themselves on their flesh" (Revelation 19:11-21).

All people have a curiosity about the future. That's a fact. But strangely, many of those same individuals seem to have an aversion about warnings related to what's ahead. Consider Noah, whom 2 Peter 2:5 calls **"a preacher of righteousness."** Presumably, people gradually heard the news that a great deluge was coming, yet the vast majority chose to ignore this message from God. The response of

Noah and his family, however, was different. They put faith in what the Lord said.

If our day is similar to that of Noah, then a good source for gaining wisdom about preparing for the last days is to review what happened back then. The Bible says, **"By faith Noah, when warned about things not yet seen, in holy fear built an ark to save his family"** (Hebrews 11:7).

The **first** factor that motivated Noah to prepare himself and his family was <u>his faith</u>. <u>He chose to heed God's warning!</u> It takes a powerful faith to work on a huge ark when all your neighbors call you crazy. What a strong family this must have been to go about constructing this massive floating zoo, and then gather all the creatures to fill it. This project took them many years to complete.

HOLY FEAR

There is a **second** important element about Noah's preparation. He stepped out in faith with an attitude of <u>holy fear</u>. This is critical! Holy fear is what motivates people to adhere to God's standards above all else. My wife and I chose to believe the divine warning we received in 1971 about America becoming the superpower of Revelation 13, and doing so gave us a holy fear in our walk with the Lord.

Hebrews 11:7a says, **"By faith Noah, when warned about things not yet seen, in holy fear built an ark to save his family."** He trusted in God completely. Obedience was foremost in Noah's mind because he had a proper fear of the Lord. This same attitude will keep us in these last days and help save Christianity in America.

"Learn to <u>fear</u> the Lord your God" (Deuteronomy 31:12). **"The Lord confides in those who <u>fear</u> him"** (Psalm 25:14). **"But the eyes of the Lord are on those who <u>fear</u> him"** (Psalm 33:18). **"The angel of the Lord encamps around those who <u>fear</u> him, and He delivers them"** (Psalm 34:7). **"For those who <u>fear</u> him lack nothing"** (Psalm 34:9). **"Through the <u>fear</u> of the Lord a man avoids evil"** (Proverbs 16:6). **"To <u>fear</u> the Lord is to hate evil"** (Proverbs 8:13). **"He who <u>fears</u> the**

Lord has a secure fortress, and for his children it will be a refuge" (Proverbs 14:26). **"Then the church ... was strengthened; and encouraged by the Holy Spirit ... living in the <u>fear</u> of the Lord"** (Acts 9:31). **"Live your lives as strangers here in reverent fear"** (1 Peter 1:17).

To have a holy fear is to stand in awe of and have a deep respect for God's holiness. This characteristic is what prompts us to avoid sin. It gives us a conscious urge to shun anything that would displease the Lord. Obedience becomes our utmost priority. A proper holy fear means seeking God's will in all things—examining every aspect of our lives in light of His Word. To be in the center of His will becomes the driving force behind our every thought and action.

> THE LORD WILL PROTECT US IF WE HAVE A HEALTHY FEAR OF THE LORD.

Holy fear nurtures the desire to subject everything in our lives to the same exacting standard: <u>Is this pleasing to God?</u> Holy fear develops a heart that is open to conviction. Holy fear gives us discernment. It allows the Lord to open our spiritual eyes.

To stay in line spiritually, we must have a proper fear of the Lord. If we don't, we will start to take our relationship with Him for granted. We will also lose our sensitivity to the influence of the world around us. All too easily we will develop spiritual pride and begin taking liberties, which not only affect our spiritual walk but hurt others. Without holy fear, our hearts quickly become hypocritical. We stop seeking righteousness.

Jesus kept His eyes on the mark. He avoided sin at every turn. He never wavered. A proper holy fear will keep us from straying from God's standards and toward the ways of the world. It will also keep us from being led astray by others who have gotten off-track.

Surely we don't possess holy fear if our standards allow us to walk along the edges of darkness. We should stay as far away as possible from worldly values and give no advantage to Satan. We must have a passion to avoid sin and to always walk in a manner pleasing to God. Those who have a holy fear have nothing to be afraid of in the days to come, regardless of what happens. Great courage against the enemy begins with a proper holy fear of the Lord. According to Scripture, the Lord will protect us, regardless of the circumstances, if we have a <u>healthy fear of the Lord</u>.

It is most unfortunate that godly fear no longer characterizes America. In many ways it has disappeared from the church as well. In a time not that unlike our own, Noah stood out as being different. Putting obedience to God's directive above all else, he prepared those closest to him for events that would mean the destruction of everyone else. This same attitude needs to mark the behavior of those who wish to live a decidedly Christian life in today's world. It's what I call "building spiritual arks of safety."

PERSONAL EXAMPLE

I have shared that in the fall of 1969, the Lord directed my wife and me to take into our home six children whose parents had tragically been killed in an automobile accident. Being somewhat overwhelmed by this sudden increase in responsibility, we depended on the Lord to lead us in raising our expanded family.

Soon God began to open our eyes to Satan's deceptive attacks. Through various prophetic Scriptures, the Lord showed us why Satan would be as successful as he has been in overcoming Christians in our country. By faith we chose to believe what the Lord was revealing to us. The fruit of our society in recent decades clearly shows that what the Lord showed us has now come to pass. Insight from the Lord about these Scriptures gave us the materials we needed to build our own spiritual ark as we raised nine godly children in an increasingly godless society.

I have written seven books, plus booklets and newsletters, about the spiritual warfare going on. In addition, I have served several years as an elder and teacher at my church. In 1974 my wife and I founded Paradise Valley Christian School in Phoenix, Arizona serving all Christian denominations (www.paradisevalleychristian.org). In 1991, we founded

Christian Life Outreach, which publishes Christian materials and runs Help The World Direct, a missionary outreach for the needy in Kenya, East Africa. In 1998, we founded Golden Eagle Christian Center, a fully equipped retreat center in Palestine, Ohio. Both of these ministries can be found at www.bobfraleychristainlifeoutreach.com. My employment has been in the aluminum industry, mostly as an executive. In 1997 I founded my own manufacturing company, ALEXCO, which produces high-tech aluminum extruded alloys for the aerospace industry (www.alexcoaz.com). Recently I was challenged by the Lord to start a campaign on a much larger scale than anything in our past. Its purpose was to share the spiritual warfare principles the Lord has been teaching me and my wife for decades. I call this effort Campaign Save America (www.campaignsaveamerica.com).

I mention these things to show how the Lord can work through lives once we have been set free from our bondage to the ways of the world. Not one of these efforts has been a burden to our family. In truth, we have experienced miraculous blessings all along the way, and they continue to happen!

As you can see by our example, we are not to remove ourselves from the world, but to live the Christian life as best as we can within its dominion. It is normal to want to take ourselves out of Satan's realm of influence. However, that is not the answer. We are to follow the principles taught in the Bible that teach us how to live in the world, but not be a part of its ways.

There is no set "ark-building" formula for everyone. All of us individually need to know the mind of the Lord, especially in these times of heavy spiritual warfare. I can, however, share with you an important word the Lord gave me about the times in which we live: FEAR NOT THE DAYS TO COME, BUT FEAR THIS ONLY: THAT YOU WALK IN A MANNER PLEASING TO THE LORD.

My own assignments have been much easier than what the Lord asked of Noah. Even so, I believe I am living at a time when God is once again warning people about the near future. Because of this, I have experienced the same frustration I'm sure Noah did—trying to point out to people what's ahead, only to see them respond with indifference or mockery. Nevertheless, I have known a great sense of fulfillment working on these "ark projects" assigned to me by the Lord.

"Building spiritual arks of safety" also includes protecting those we love by encouraging them to make obedience to the Lord their number-one priority. That's one of the reasons I wrote this book. Even if I were to die suddenly, my loved ones would still know what I believed and how it showed itself in my life. This book makes that plain. It's what Barbara and I have come to embrace through our four decades of following Jesus together. If anyone wonders what the two of us are passionate about in our Christian walk, the answer is in these pages.

Is everything I have written correct down to the last detail? I can't say with absolute certainty. But the broad strokes are so much a part of what we believe that we have patterned our entire lives around them.

OTHER EXAMPLES

Your experience will differ from ours. I'm sure that in many ways some of you have passed us spiritually in what you have learned. Therefore, we sincerely want to hear what God has taught you. Even today, how are you preparing for the future? Testimonies from people like you are an integral part of Campaign Save America. This Web site (www.bob fraleychristianlifeoutreach.com) is a place where we can learn from one another how God is growing us in our faith, especially in these times when it looks like the coming of the Lord is not that far off. People can read how others are preparing for those closest to them to be able to stand strong in the world of both today and tomorrow. That's what "spiritual arks of safety" are about.

Here is what one person wrote: *At our church I was challenged to write out a list of my present 5- and 10-year prayer requests for the people I love the most. This assignment changed my prayer life from what I now realize was a somewhat superficial approach to one of becoming a real prayer warrior on behalf of my family and close friends. This single exercise*

*also got me started in keeping a prayer notebook, which has had a pro-
found effect on my walk with the Lord, and given me a deeper love than
I ever could have imagined for those I pray for.*

CONCLUDING THOUGHTS

When I examine the spiritual development of America, it's obvious
that God has a special calling, for America. Human wisdom alone did
not develop our country. Men inspired by God were at the core of
every aspect of our nation's early formation. I believe that except for
Israel, God has never intervened in a country's spiritual development
as much as He has in this nation's.

My conviction is that the Lord has a special calling for America in
our days. Generally speaking, His mission for these end-times is for us
to be the "salt of the earth" and the "light of the world." Unfortunately,
the enemy has deceived many in the American church in recent generations, and our fruit reveals that we have fallen away from our calling,
leaving our nation spiritually vulnerable. But as my brother testifies,
though he was deceived, he was restored and experienced a personal
revival, and was still able to fulfill his original calling. I am convinced
this principle can also apply to the American church. There is a lot of
discussion about revival in the Body of Christ, but it will take a spirit
of repentance and turning from the ways of the world.

As there have been divine interventions in America's past, there is
no reason why this couldn't happen once again. I suspect the Lord is
behind some of the hard times our nation has known of late. It's His
way of trying to draw us back to Himself.

More often than not, revivals begin when times are tough. This
has certainly been the case historically in our country. You see, people
satisfied with where they are don't aspire to anything better. So when
revivals are traced back to their roots, what is found is a deep-seated
longing for something better than what is presently being experienced.
In a day when the enemy is strutting around like Goliath of old, a great
sense of unrest begins to mark a growing number of God's people.

Those experiencing this holy unrest over the religious status quo are far different from the church's chronic complainers. Ministers need to be aware of and discerning about this. The complainers are a drain on any congregation, but the "restless ones" can be the key to future revival. Like several godly women in Scripture, they are crying out, "Don't let me die barren, Lord!" This is what the first revival prayers sound like when God begins to work among His people. In a day in which evil is blatant, certain of God's servants must carry the burden of an intense spiritual dissatisfaction.

Has this been happening to you? You are greatly troubled that society now influences the church far more than the church influences society. You bemoan the fact that so few believers' lives are characterized by spiritual victory. Your concern for revival in your church, town or country has almost become overwhelming.

> HE WAS RESTORED AND EXPERIENCED A PERSONAL REVIVAL.

Yet, sometimes if you are someone who is called to get up to teach a class or preach, you feel so ineffectual. It's as though no matter what you say, it's not going to be enough. At times you even have a sense of sobbing, "Lord, have mercy! Lord, have mercy!" Consider the possibility that what you're experiencing is a deep sense of dissatisfaction.

All across the country, there are believers having trouble holding back their tears. Some could probably identify with Jeremiah's feelings as he thought about the sins of his people: **"Oh, that my head were a spring of water and my eyes a fountain of tears!"** (Jeremiah 9:1). They find themselves troubled about the future of their communities, their nation and the world. They're not confident that they have the ability to do much to help turn things around.

If this is where you are, you should know that you're not alone. The Lord is burdening many believers in the same way. It's in line with how revival normally unfolds. The truth is, what you're experiencing is not that unusual. It's where the process normally begins. So, welcome to the ranks of the discontent. It's an honor to be divinely chosen. In the long run, it can be very good for you, your church, your country and the world.

It's foolish to try to fit God into a box. He can do what He wants in whatever way most pleases Him. Anyone who studies revival history knows this to be true. Even so, a careful look at past revivals makes it possible to see a sequence of events that often unfolds. A discernible pattern can prove helpful for us today—as long as we don't try to set it in stone, religiously speaking.

A CORE GROUP COMMITTED TO PRAYER IS NEEDED.

What begins with a deep dissatisfaction regarding the way things are, needs to move toward a *concerted prayer effort*. This longing for something better has to become a sustained hope. Otherwise, the frustration of delay has a tendency to lead to burnout and bitterness. It would be difficult to pinpoint a time during which God has poured out His Spirit without someone, somewhere, paying the price in prayer. This commitment to prayer is not a casual effort, though. It involves long seasons of intercession.

Prayer is the power source for revival. Armin Gesswein writes in his book *With One Accord in One Place*: *"Most churches are said to fail because they do not generate their own power. This is also true of the individual Christian. Prayer is the generator. The great London preacher Charles Spurgeon once took some people down to his Metropolitan Tabernacle basement to show them his 'power plant.' There, on their knees, were about three hundred people praying for the service!"*

This is a good illustration because concerted prayer efforts usually require partnerships, or group prayer. The burden is too heavy, the calling too difficult and the enemy too strong for any one individual to stand in the gap alone. A core group of believers seriously committed to prayer is needed if a vision of revival is to come alive. The phrase "core group" doesn't necessarily mean that a large number of people is required. Initially, it may be just a handful in a church, on a campus, or scattered throughout a denomination—determined people willing to be involved in a prayer ministry. In other words, they won't be easily discouraged, but will continue to pray until God answers.

Using the words of Scripture can be a powerful way to plead for revival. Bible verses may be prayed back to God in this way:

"Restore us again, O God our Savior, and put away your displeasure toward us. Will you be angry with us forever? Will you prolong your anger through all generations? Will you not revive us again, that your people may rejoice in you?" (Psalm 85:4-6)

"Let your hand rest on the man at your right hand, the son of man you have raised up for yourself. Then we will not turn away from you; revive us, and we will call on your name" (Psalm 80:17-18).

Teams devoted to prayer should remind themselves of how the Lord has worked in the past. For example, they may recall how He rescued the Jews when Queen Esther called for three days of intense prayer and fasting. As they do this, the conviction grows in their hearts that someday soon the Lord will also honor the earnest prayers of His people in this generation.

For far too long a lack of prayer was one of the greatest weaknesses in the church. Christians acted as if they were resourceful enough to move the cause of Jesus Christ forward without much help from Him. But thankfully, that day is changing! One of the great signs of the times is a growing prayer movement. I doubt it's reached the proportions it needs to, but it's ever-expanding. Nothing could be a more positive message of better days ahead. Building a strong prayer base and anticipating that it will result in revival is a lesson we can learn from history. It doesn't try to force God into a box, and it certainly puts the church in an advantageous position.

God's Word gives us a framework for national revival in 2 Chronicles 7:14. He says: **"If my people, who are called by my name, will humble themselves and pray and seek my face and turn from their**

wicked ways, then I will hear from heaven and forgive their sins and will heal their land.”

This is exactly the pattern followed by my brother, Dr. Fraley. He humbled himself, sought the face of the Lord, repented and turned from the sin in which he was involved, and the Lord spiritually healed him. Please notice this verse states “if <u>my</u> people.” It is the people of God who must follow these instructions. This is not a calling to the people of the world. If we as Christians are willing to humble ourselves, pray, seek the Lord's face and renounce the ways of the world, the Lord will surely restore America's Christian heritage and make our country safe for another generation or two.

FINAL WORDS

I am in my seventies. My eyes are not as strong as they used to be. My spiritual sight, however, has improved with age. I see the beast of Revelation 13 more clearly now than I did when I was at my prime, physically speaking.

Though I have not had a vision like my brother did, I can easily envision this beast he told me about. It continues to feed on believers as it looms over our nation. I am passionate in my desire to battle against it. That is obviously a bigger job than any one person can accomplish on his or her own; nevertheless, I do all within my power to make people aware of its diabolical presence.

All this could result in living with an ongoing nightmare, were it not for the fact that my eyes are fixed on Jesus. His presence is quite real to me. He fills my days in such a wonderful way that my focus is completely on Him; He has been remarkably gracious. I am most thankful that all those in my immediate family love and serve Him. They are in our “spiritual ark of safety.” Thank You Jesus!

Having finished this book, I'm sure some might say my warning is little more than foolishness. Others may see my interpretations as skewed. I admit there is a part of me that hopes what I have written about America and her future is wrong. But ever since the Lord inspired me to explore this possibility of America becoming a backslidden America and the beast / superpower John saw in the last days, there is nothing in my research and study of Scripture and history that would diminish this prophetic truth.

Scripture makes it plain that the Jewish nation that experienced first-hand the presence of God, witnessed His miracles and blessings, became so deceived by this clever enemy called Satan that they totally missed the incarnation, when God became man and visited planted earth.

Has Satan, masquerading as an angel of light, once again used deception to fool huge numbers into thinking the beast / superpower he is working through has to be some other religion or power, when in reality, it's the country that has been the center of Christianity and many times called "Christian America" that he has his sights set on as we near the second coming of Jesus?

Certainly one of my repeated prayers is that the churches of this land will know another powerful move of God's Spirit that will bring about an era of holiness and divine protection. No one finds pleasure in pointing out where our defenses are weak.

I am also aware that, like all my brothers and sisters, I am flawed. None of us, looking back over the years, can say we always lived as we should. But God in His incredible kindness and mercy has allowed us the privilege of experiencing Christ and sharing in His ongoing work. Maybe we will even be a part of that privileged generation of stewards on duty when our master makes His triumphant return!

QUESTIONS FOR GROUP DISCUSSION AND/OR TO BE ANSWERED INDIVIDUALLY

What does "holy fear" mean to you, and how do you see it relating to your life?

_____

_____

_____

_____

_____

_____

_____

Define what it means for someone to "build a spiritual ark of safety."

_____

_____

_____

_____

_____

_____

I have shared how my wife and I responded in faith to what God asked us to do. What would you list as acts of faith in your life?

_____

_____

_____

_____

_____

_____

What has been your personal experience in terms of praying for revival?

_____

_____

_____

_____

_____

_____

_____

_____

Who are some people you might consider asking to join you in praying for spiritual awakening in America?

_____

_____

_____

_____

_____

_____

_____

How will your life be different as a result of reading this book?

_____

_____

_____

_____

_____

_____

_____

BIOGRAPHY: BOB FRALEY

Bob Fraley is a Christian leader, educator and author, who for more than 35 years has been teaching and writing to help open the eyes of believers to the spiritual attacks of the enemy on America. Bob has also had a long and successful career in the corporate business world. He defines America as that country God raised up to be Salt and Light—the center of Christianity—in these last days. However, just as Satan often caused the Jewish nation to fall away, he now has his eyes set on destroying "Christian America."

In his research Bob discovered that most Christians in America are not spiritually prepared to stand against Satan's deceptive tactics being used in his end-time warfare against Christianity in our country. Bob's ministry, "Christian Life Outreach," initiated a 'Campaign to Save America,' by teaching Christians how to build a spiritual ark of protection for their families so they can spiritually survive and excel in these last days, fulfilling God's mission for Christians to be Salt and Light.

His teaching is taught from personal experience, not just book knowledge. He and his wife Barbara have been married for 52 years and have raised 9 children. They have an incredible life story to tell. In 1969 he and his wife were prompted by the Lord to take six children and raise them along with their own, when the children's parents were killed in an automobile accident.

In 1971 Bob had a revolutionary encounter with the Lord about the prophetic times in which we live. He was shown how Satan would attack to destroy Christian America in these last days, which would have a devastating effect on American families and our country's moral values. This caused Bob and his wife to become very dependent on the Lord to teach them how to raise their expanded family. The Lord inspired Bob to study the Scriptures about the end-times and the Christian walk along with researching America's spiritual history so he and his wife could prepare their family for the spiritual warfare the enemy would be conducting.

Soon thereafter the Lord convicted Bob that he was to share the biblical principles that he was learning about this spiritual warfare in these last days. His first book was published in 1975. As he grew in his understanding He continued to write and has now had seven books and several booklets published. His latest book, *You Are Salt & Light*, is a summary of the biblical principles he has learned over the years.

The Fraley's testimony confirms Bob's message. They have not had any of the contemporary problems—drugs, alcohol, divorce, rebellion, etc.—with their children or grandchildren and most of them were very active in school and college. Their family has grown to 62 members and continues to grow. They all—except the few who are still too young—have made a commitment to serve the Lord.

For more than 35 years Bob has been attempting to both open the eyes of fellow believers and to help equip them to spiritually survive and excel in these critical end-times. What the Lord showed Bob back in 1971 about the spiritual warfare that would be taking place in America has all come true. Long time friends and colleagues all acknowledge that he was right about his message. Never in the history of mankind has a society changed its moral values so drastically in such a short period of time as Americans have in the past generation.

In 2007 Bob Fraley found prominent support for his message: Dr. David Mains. Dr. Mains is a well-known Christian Leader in America, serving as senior pastor in Chicago at Circle Church for ten years and then as director of the Chapel of the Air radio ministry for two decades. In 1995 the National Religious Broadcasters honored him with their Television Program of the Year award. Dr. Mains and Bob Fraley have developed a new teaching series about the last days titled, "The Remarkable Revelation: 50 Days to Prepare for What's Ahead."

Bob has written 7 books, various booklets, and recently produced a DVD of a television interview of him and David Mains. He is now ready to start a consistent Strategic Campaign to spread his message about these last days that is shared in his latest book, *You Are Salt & Light*.

BOB FRALEY CHRISTIAN LIFE OUTREACH ACTIVITIES AND OFFERINGS

1. INDIVIDUAL BOOKS:

- You Are Salt & Light
- The Day that Changed America
- Holy Fear
- Prepare Yourself
- Caught in the Web of Deception by Dr. Charles Fraley
  with Bob Fraley
- Last Days in America

Individual Booklets:

- A Time for Action
- Campaign Save Christian America
- Could You be Caught in the Web of Deception
- It Will be Worth It All / Si Vale La Pena

2. 'THE REMARKABLE REVELATION' BY DR. DAVID MAINS AND BOB FRALEY:

- 2 DVDs with 19 Sermon Manuscripts, Powerpoints and Graphics for Preaching and Teaching:
  - * Audio Visual Tools include Drama and Word on the Street Clips
  - * Promotion & Implementation Tools
  - * Success for Leadership Training Video
- 2 Books: 'You Are Salt & Light', 'The Day that Changed America'.
- 1 Adult Bible Study Journal

! Request a FREE introductory DVD with Dr. David Mains and Bob Fraley !

3. **HELP THE WORLD:** A **missionary outreach** that helps the poor and needy in Africa. This outreach is unique in that 100% of all donations go to help those in need. There are no salaries or administration expenses.

4. **GOLDEN EAGLE CHRISTIAN CENTER:** A fully equipped **Christian retreat center** in Ohio that churches and Christian groups from all denominations use for training and fellowship retreats.

5. **CAMPAIGN SAVE AMERICA:** An **outreach to share the Scriptural principles** the Lord has been teaching Bob and his wife since the early 1970s that will guide Christians to be spiritually equipped to live victoriously and be Salt & Light in these last days.

OTHER POINTS OF INTEREST:

In 1974 Bob and Barbara founded Paradise Valley Christian School in Phoenix, Arizona, which today is one of the major Christian schools in the Phoenix area serving all Christian denominations (www.paradisevalleychristian.org).

Bob's career has been in the aluminum industry where he has served at the executive level of management. In 1997, he founded his own company, ALEXCO, a manufacturing company that produces high tech aluminum extruded alloys for the aerospace industry (www.alexcoaz.com).

To order books and DVDs or to find out more about 'Bob Fraley Christian Life Outreach', please visit our website @ www.bobfraleychristianlifeoutreach.com or call us @ 866 998 4136 or e-mail, xnlifeout@yahoo.com.